UP PERISCOPE

PUTTING TRADITIONAL LEADERSHIP IN THE CROSSHAIRS

UP PERISCOPE

PUTTING TRADITIONAL LEADERSHIP IN THE CROSSHAIRS

DEBORAH CAKE FORTIN, MS
JOHN GREGORY VINCENT, MBA

Columbus, Ohio

UP PERISCOPE: Putting Traditional Leadership in the Crosshairs

Published by Gatekeeper Press
2167 Stringtown Rd, Suite 109
Columbus, OH 43123-2989
www.GatekeeperPress.com

ISBN (hardcover): 9781642379617
eISBN: 9781642379624

TESTIMONIALS

"I have known Deb and John for many years now and have come to respect and admire their views on leadership. Their systematic approach to leading through embracing diversity and inclusion with a commitment to developing new leaders in any organization is simply teaching leadership principles the right way. *Up Periscope* is a must read for emerging and established leaders who are focused on both improving their bottom line and the lives of those they serve through the process of becoming better leaders."

—Deke Copenhaver
Best Selling Author of *The Changemaker:
the Art of Building Better Leaders*
Former Mayor, City of Augusta, Georgia

"Finally, a book for ALL LEADERS!
"Many books on leadership focus on upper management, forgetting that the middle will make the biggest difference. *Up Periscope* focuses on teaching ALL LEVELS of management to be more inclusive and effective, a step-by-step guide to be able to achieve more successful management skills. I also like the focus on 'non-title' leadership, those natural-born leaders who take control, helping them find a way to use their talents as well. Teaching man-

agers to focus on the mission and use each team members' skills to achieve this mission sounds redundant, in reality this is a much-needed teaching. Excited to put what I learn into practice."

—Maya Barbery
D&I Practitioner

"Experience provides the lens through which I evaluate the effectiveness of current and future decisions. This lens provides me with passion and strength; it defines principles; it yields discernment. However, these experiences (and my textbook knowledge) are woefully inadequate to effectively guide, mentor and grow new, better leaders. Experiences have to be coupled with a systemic approach that ensures sustainment and reproducibility – an approach that makes it 'the way we do business.' This way, when I move on to my next experience, the new leaders can build on these blocks. John and Deb in *Up Periscope* so effectively present the core building blocks of that system – a system that resources and strengthens people to solve incredibly complex problems, innovate, learn, and create value for the organization, themselves, and society."

—Cheryl R. Hild PhD
Graduate School of Business, Lincoln Memorial University

"*Up Periscope* fills a niche for Leaders who are looking to develop themselves and strengthen their team. John synthesizes the complexity of leadership, inclusiveness and diversity into an easy to digest strategy that is applicable immediately. He transforms the secrets of Submarine life into tools that can be quickly instituted in any situation with the focus on accountability, communication, and continuous improvement and development at all levels. This is a must have book in the arsenal of leadership.

—Nadia Vicente
Product Adoption Manager, American
Consumer Healthcare Tech at GSK

"As an Airman who has served over 24 years in the U.S. Air Force and achieved the top enlisted rank of chief master sergeant (the top 1% of the enlisted force), I have led many Airmen (civilian and military) within many organizations around the globe. I have led these Airmen in times of peace but mostly in times of war. Accordingly, I know the uncompromising importance of mission success and organizational effectiveness. Our families, communities and country-at-large depend heavily on the U.S. Armed Forces (Army, Navy, Air Force, Marines, Coast Guard and the newly created Space Force) as a whole to defend our sovereignty and our way of life . . . and rightfully so! For the Armed Forces and national defense and security agencies to do so, many things must be done "the right way": 1. The right people must be chosen and the team must be properly trained; 2. Effective intra-agency and inter-agency communication and collaboration must be present and optimal; 3. A mission-focused mindset must be established with each employee having "buy-in" into the company's objectives and goals; 4. Last, but most importantly, the right organizational culture must be sought and established.

"Without organizations creating the right culture (a culture of innovation and inclusiveness that values learning and its people), none of the first three essential things mentioned above will stand. Like a three-legged chair needing a fourth leg, so must the fourth principle be present for an organization to be successful. It is the organizational culture that "steers the ship" when it comes to what kind of employees should be hired, how inclusiveness is established and integrated throughout the company, and what values are upheld and are nonnegotiable.

"In this profound book, Deb and John provide practical ways every organization must do to be successful (effective) at achieving its goals. From giving 'Five Anchors of Leadership' to arming leaders with a tried and true 'Methodology' that creates a culture that values people and increases the bottom line, *Up Periscope: Putting Traditional Leadership in the Crosshairs* is a piece I highly recommend any leader (civilian or military) add to his/her repertoire of scholastic collections. By doing so, you will harness the tools you need to structure your organization the 'right way' . . . the 'Submarine Way' . . . and thereby increase its ROI."

—CMSgt Rodney P. Huffman, M.Min., PMP, PMC

In addition to serving in the U.S. Air Force, Rodney Huffman is also an ordained minister of 25 years who has conducted global ministry and established three churches within the U.S.

"An exceptional perspective to creating and fostering inclusive leadership. Deb and John's unique journeys demonstrate how leadership lives outside the walls of titles and dives deep into creating an atmosphere of leadership development for all."

—Christine Sanni
Author of *Meet Me At The Table*; Coach, CEO ConservGeo

"I was first introduced to John when he was an early guest lecturer for The Honor Foundation - an executive-level transition fellowship for special operations personnel. He was enthusiastic, candid, and colorful, exactly what one would expect from a well-versed and salty retired Command Master Chief. His background allowed him to easily penetrate the veneer of our skeptical crowd, who were transiting unknown waters for the first in a very long time. Not only did he enlighten us as to the meaning of our Gallup CliftonStrengths assessments, but he also taught us how to capitalize on them through the power of being 'pointy.' With their first book, *[Diversity and Inclusion] The Submarine Way*, John and Deb created a how-to manual on creating diversity and inclusion in any work environment through the employment of 'The System.' The ladder rungs of 'The System' lead to one thing - Focus on the Mission, which, as a United States Marine Raider, is a focus I live by. But even with measured employment of 'The System,' an organization still requires the leadership to pull it all together, enter *Up Periscope*. With *Up Periscope*, John and Deb have written an amazing companion piece to *The Submarine Way*. Here they give us the 'anchors' of leadership development that when applied with 'The System,' equal organizational success. In Marine special operations, it's necessary we accelerate the leadership development of our Raiders who experience diverse and ambiguous challenges early in their careers. Deb and John's 'anchors' provide a solid framework to do just that, some of which I knew instinctively and some of which I never considered. *Up Periscope* is a must-read for leaders, especially those who want to experience the view from a new lens and to learn the power of being 'pointy.'

— Garret Harrell
Marine Raider | Adaptive Leader | Team Builder |
Creative Problem Solver | Hair Metal Enthusiast

FOREWORD

I met John Gregory Vincent on submarines in the mid-'90s. I was fortunate enough to be invited to go underway on the USS *L. Mendel Rivers* several times as a civilian guest, or "rider" as the crew liked to refer to us. There, the leadership John speaks about in this book, along with the camaraderie, support, and sarcasm, was certainly evident. What really struck me was that from the Commanding Officer, Captain Brad McDonald, to the seaman who washes dishes, the level of understanding of the mission and their role in it, as well as their commitment to the successful completion of it ,was beyond anything I'd ever experienced.

I saw 110 sailors, many in their late teens and early twenties, become a cohesive group, a crew. Hyper-focused on the mission and working together collaboratively to successfully complete nearly impossible missions. Teaching others how to develop leaders like this is important. It was important for me personally. I took away many life lessons that I still refer to and use today. This book is a unique view into the secret world of submarines and those sailors who safeguard our way of life. John and Deb have surfaced many powerful and completely unique lessons and techniques that every person in any type of leadership role will benefit from.

—H Wayne Huizenga, Jr.
President, Huizenga Holdings, Inc.
CEO of Rybovich a Superyacht Facility

ABOUT THE AUTHORS

Deb is the founder and president of The Submarine Way. Her passion for inclusion and her experience as an executive in Fortune 500 companies allowed her to take the leadership system found on submarines and apply it to businesses and organizations to better position them for inclusive environments.

John spent fourteen of his twenty years in the Navy on submarines. There he learned the powerful lessons of leadership development and inclusion. Post-Navy, John joined Gallup, Inc. and became one of Gallup's top global consultants. Today, John is the principal consultant and keynote speaker for The Submarine Way.

Contact us through thesubmarineway@gmail.com, or contact us through the website www.thesubmarineway.com

PREFACE

There are many leadership books written from the viewpoint of Navy admirals, Marine and Army generals, and commanding officers of all varieties. I have read many of them and love a few. This book is not written from that viewpoint. My leadership was forged through the eyes of a career enlisted. Approached and encouraged, even, starting my second year of Naval service on submarines, to "do better and become an officer," I chose time and time again to remain an enlisted service member. My view out the periscope is that of a leader who realized the unparalleled leadership impact of a strong senior enlisted, what many in the private sector would refer to as a mid-level to director-level manager. Every organization is a pyramid, a few people at the top, the majority at or near the entry, to lower-level positions. The unique application of leadership through the laser lens of a Command Master Chief is this: only a Command Master Chief has complete relatability to the most junior person in the organization and can also get a short notice face-to-face with the Admiral.

When I was in the submarine force, very early on, I knew I was not motivated by power. I also knew I was big thinking with big thinking strategies. I needed to build skills in areas of talent, and I needed to have the authority to carry those ideas out. I have built my consulting company around this view and the belief in the influence and critical importance of these leaders. I now consult and coach executives from Fortune 50 companies and lead discussions with entry-level team leaders. The tools and perspective from my periscope are completely unique, based on this experience as well as my time with Gallup as a consultant. I respected Gallup over the years as a sailor from the outside, never imagining I would be on the inside as a consultant, becoming their top client-rated consultant in the world. The combination of this strength-based view, the System learned on submarines, the Methodology, and Process (patent pending) will become staples in the seabags of executives and first-time supervisors alike. Why? Well, I don't just remember what it is like to clean a toilet; I still do on occasion.

CONTENTS

Testimonials 5

Foreword.. 11

About The Authors 13

Preface... 15

Acknowledgment.. 19

Introduction 21

Chapter 1   If One does not Know to Which Port
            One is Sailing, No Wind is Favorable 27

Chapter 2   Anchor 1: Fighting the Submarine
            takes a Crew-munity 39

Chapter 3   Anchor 2: Captains are Willing to go
            Down with the Ship.. 53

Chapter 4   Anchor 3: Who is your Sea Daddy? 63

Chapter 5   Anchor 4: It is not the Ship, so much
            as the Skillful Sailing that Assures a
            Prosperous Voyage 87

Chapter 6   Anchor 5: Crew-munity Starts with Crew 99

Chapter 7   When the Sails Find Perfect Winds 116

Chapter 8   When Leading is Difficult 129

Chapter 9   Sailing Your Own Ship 138

Chapter 10 Sailor's Knot.. 149

ACKNOWLEDGMENT

First and foremost, to Deb Cake Fortin, my best friend, business partner, wife and animal whisperer: I continue to learn from you daily. My respect, love and devotion will last forever.

There are so many great leaders who have influenced us over the years: Drew Griffin, a progressive (not intended in the political sense) southern city manager; Deke Copenhaver, the former mayor of Augusta, GA, who has so much to say about leadership that he wrote his own book. Yes, there were plenty of leaders along the way we didn't want to be like, and yes, ironically, we thank them, too.

Brad McDonald deserves special recognition. He was John's most impactful Commanding Officer and remains a mentor and dear friend to this day. Carey Mason was Deb's mentor and friend at ADP and provided thoughtful guidance throughout the publishing of our first book. Liz Brown was (and is) a trailblazer when the choices for women were limited, especially coming from a traditional family where she bumped up against the status quo more than once. She started out in corporate America, achieved success, and went on to own her own marketing company. Thank you to the first female submariners. All of you have paved the way for submariners and continue to lead the rest of us with your strength, toughness, and determination.

These are the leaders who, in a quiet way, small way or a big way, but in their own unique way, make a difference in their worlds. They are fair, believe in equity, live it every day, and change the world a person, neighborhood, or boat at a time. These leaders are part of the symphony of leaders we refer to so often in this book. True leadership is not a relentless drive of one person's will, but the ability to discern when another should lead, when your role as a leader is to augment someone else, and even when to turn around and change direction. True leaders put their biases in their seabags and leave them there. There's no room for bias in leadership, no room at all.

To all these leaders, the present and future leaders reading this book and the others we haven't mentioned, fair winds and following seas to you all.

USS *L. MENDEL RIVERS* (SSN 686)
Where my passion for lifelong leadership development began

INTRODUCTION

Leadership, The Submarine Way

Most leaders learn how to get other's actions aligned with their goals. They/we learn how to manage the performance of those who are not performing to standards. Occasionally, we stumble on some teamwork techniques that work, and when we are lucky, we will have a team. A complete contrarian approach to leadership will be described here:

- First, appreciate the individual. Why spend considerable time and energy managing negative performance when you can build on talents, what people are naturally best at, and then get people's roles aligned with these talents and manage the individual in an area so much more effectively?
- Then, when the individual is engaged, work on each team member so they contribute by building their talents to strengths.
- Encourage the individual, set goals for the team, support them and spend time on negative performance only if it

affects the performance of the individual, the team, or the organization.

- Drive inclusion through appreciating the strengths of every individual and tolerate no outward bias from the team. You will see engagement and inclusion from the team in measurable ways.

It is not a simple formula, but it can be done if you follow the Five Anchors of Leadership, the methodology, the System, and the process found here. Enjoy reading this innovative view of leadership, and we promise you this: as a leader, we will touch your soul, and it will be tough to return to the traditional leadership model you likely learned.

My Story

I can still remember, like it was just yesterday, the day when my feet hit the steel deck that first time. I looked around, and my first thought was, "You've got to be kidding me; this is too small." They don't let us on submarines during sub school, and it didn't take me long to figure out why. We spent our time on simulators when I got on my first boat, but not during sub school itself. Nothing could have prepared me for this anyway. So small, with people everywhere. The smell hit me almost simultaneously, and I thought, how can I tolerate this smell for a whole deployment? You see, the desalination equipment (a system that turns seawater into drinking water) was down more than up, and 110 unwashed bodies and their unwashed clothes can become malodorous.

Old, for a brand-new sailor at 22, I didn't realize those first few months of smell, attitude, pressure from the Chiefs, pressure from the hull (we were 800 feet under the ocean), with limited space would set the stage for building resilience, and yes, even leadership, that would build character for a lifetime. Unlike most of my peers, I came to the Navy with considerable sea time. I attended a maritime college until I was thrown out for partying too much, so I then did sea time in the Merchant Marines until I figured out what was next. After two years with them, spending time with a scary band of brothers that I fit in with way too well, I joined the Navy. My passion for the ocean was all-consuming. Growing up on Long Island, it was always there, her presence, her beauty, and allure. A fascination for navigation got me to experience navigating with the Merchant Marines using the stars and a sextant along with some basic electronics tools, which set the stage for a move to Assistant Navigator at meteoric speed, but that's a story for another time.

Writing a book on leadership is as natural to me as wearing a Navy uniform or hitting the mountain bike trails. In fact, many years later, it still fits (the uniform that is). Leadership still fits, too. I speak about it, consult, coach, and train it. Are leaders made or born? The answer is yes. Deb, my business partner, wife, and co-author, was a natural leader who started managing and leading people at 23. We had all the right instincts, but we needed development. Neither one of us had developed in the way leaders are developed today. We watched what we didn't like and avoided it. We also observed what we did and learned how to make it fit us. This set the stage for a desire to build good leaders in others. Leaders that are inclusive, and leaders that build leadership in others, in everyone. That is The Submarine Way.

When did I know I was capable of leading? It was long before I knew how important the Fouled Anchor would be to me, or any of the other leaders who lived by its creed. More to follow on that. This screw-up, a hard-headed, college throw-out felt leadership all around me from Day One in the Navy, and I felt compelled to contribute and have others look up to me—yes, me. By the time the

Fouled Anchor had been introduced to me, I wanted to lead, and I wanted to be respected.

As I mentioned in the preface, there have been many other leadership books written by captains, admirals, and other officers. I coach and work with organizations at the highest level—CEOs, COOs, and VPs—but I also work with the beat cop and the person supervising on the manufacturing floor of a high tech company or a manager/nurse in the healthcare industry. I've cleaned toilets and been a mess cook. I have a vantage point that is unique and relatable to all levels.

See, the Fouled Anchor is the emblem of the Chief Petty Officer of the US Navy. In terms of the Chief, the fouled anchor symbolizes the trials and tribulations that every Chief Petty Officer must endure daily. Attached to the anchor is a length of chain and the letters USN. To the average person, this means the United States Navy; but to a Chief, it is a Brotherhood and Sisterhood that holds leadership and heart in equal stead. The USN stands for Unity, Service, and Navigation. Navigation on a true course before God and mankind. To say we took it to heart is to underestimate the significance of the Fouled Anchor.

Meeting Kelly Baker

My first real experience with a leader who had a heart happened on my first few days on my first submarine. The Commanding Officer, or CO, was Kelly Baker. He was a kind, huge man for a submariner, and he epitomized its head and heart. My onboarding, known as a check-in on a sub, involved thirty minutes with the CO. How many people could say they spent time, within their first few days on a new job, with the CEO of the organization? This was part of the onboarding for every new crew member. I was surprisingly comfortable with this conversation. He asked me about my family, already knew about my time in the Merchant Marines and my experience with navigation. It was truly like two regular folks talking. It had an incredible impact on me, and I wanted to be a leader like him. He was modeling and coaching. I would learn later he also required us to mirror what he coached and modeled. I cannot overestimate the impact Kelly Baker had on me as a new sailor. Yes, a negative role model would have also provided a different kind of leadership, but it would have taken me much longer to figure out what kind of leader I wanted to be. Kelly laid it all out for me; he was kind, human, and interested in me, but clearly had won the respect of the crew. I had something to aim for.

For those of you not familiar with a submarine, imagine you are in a three hundred foot-long, fast attack, 637 class submarine. The 637 is the smallest in the US fleet-with about 110 sailors, eighty bunks, and no privacy. Yes, you heard it right—eighty bunks. Some of us shared bunks, what we called hot racking because with three shifts alternating on, then sleep, by the time someone new crawled in the bed, the bed was still warm from the sailor who had just rolled out it minutes before. After a while, having a bed to yourself was nice and even aspirational, but sleeping 4-5 hours in a row was rare and, therefore, much more important. Add to this: on submarines, the crew turns over every three years. Can you imagine your company, your church, or community, with the leaders and crew turning over every three years, but the mission never faltering? Did you know the average age of a submariner is 23? Ninety percent of the crew is under the age of 35, and 80% have no more formal education than a high school diploma. Yes, with all of these factors, nuclear submarines have operated in the most unpredictable environments for more than sixty years without a single accident.

The reality of life on a submarine was the best and the worst of living. There was an opportunity to show real leadership and appreciate good leaders, because it was critical to staying sane in an environment not many could fathom. Because of the close quarters, bad leaders also impacted us. Imagine a leader who is volatile, negative, and hypercritical in only 300 feet of space for over 110 people. Imagine if everyone was an inexperienced or bad leader, had little to no professional development, and no instinct for leadership, no mission focus, and no regard for people and their safety. Imagine that on a nuclear submarine.

CHAPTER 1

IF ONE DOES NOT KNOW TO WHICH PORT ONE IS SAILING, NO WIND IS FAVORABLE

The Five Anchors

Traditional leadership highlights the person at the top: the CEO, the Admiral, or four-star General. Our position is radically different. Those leaders have a role, but leadership is a symphony of leaders, where the four-star or admiral is a player, perhaps even the conductor; but depending on the situation, not even the most significant player. Without those individuals who are ready to step up, take a risk, some having a title and some not, leadership breaks down. Our goal is to build new leaders everywhere with and without formal titles. Leaders who keep their biases in a seabag and view people according to their talents and strengths (covered in chapter 5). Leaders who develop others who are fair, interdependent, and collaborative. This is not meant as a political statement, but in 2018 and 2019, the ambassadors, FBI and civil service agents who looked out for our country by stepping forward with information that could and did hurt their careers, showed leadership. The person who finally talked about what was going on the USS *Wyoming* (covered in chapter 8) showed considerable leadership.

For many of the businesses we work with, they look first at the return on investment of developing their leaders. We are comfortable and even excited with providing this data; after ten years of consulting, and three years of specific focus on inclusive leadership, the return on investment is clear and measurable. Results like a 30-50% improvement in key engagement areas, for one company; another client, an organization, was named one of the best places to work in their state; and another client, who had a low score on an employee survey, on the next survey had moved to the top tier. We have saved clients over $2,000,000 in measurable return on investment because The Submarine Way drives that symphony of leadership. Every improvement in engagement, improvement to retention, or hiring drives improvement in ROI.

What does improvement in engagement do for your organization? You could see a 20% improvement in sales, 59% reduction in turnover, and a 17% increase in productivity. What would this do for your organization in terms of revenue and achieving other financial goals? That doesn't even consider that inclusion is likely improved in your organization and that future leaders are being built. These things are not directly measurable but contribute significantly to management and organizational resiliency.

Onboarding - Setting the Stage

The onboarding (check-in) experience on a submarine sets up the new sailor for success.

> Understanding the importance of this brand-new relationship, coaching to its importance, and expecting participation from each person responsible for delivering the check-in experience, is what every official or unofficial leader of a submarine delivered.

Without a good check-in experience, new sailors would not be set up for success.

In this case, you were leading whether you had an official role as a leader or not.

The leaders, official or otherwise, who escorted me around and spent time with me during my onboarding and taught me those first few weeks set me up for success. Some of them were nice to me, like the CO I discussed earlier, and others were downright rude. I would hear that I "wasn't contributing," or I "was breathing their air," and it was not yet known how much I would contribute. Make no mistake: submarines are not places full of hugs; however, they are places full of commitment, inclusion, and hyper-focus on the mission. Bringing these things to your workplace changes everything. You will hear later about someone who wasn't pleasant (Cowboy Jim), but he was necessary for my maturity and growth as a leader. A leap in faith for anyone or anything was not a natural act on a submarine. We didn't just assume someone would figure it out eventually. Being cautious kept us alive.

Deb and I, at our consulting company, for the most part hire contractors. Despite that, we have a robust onboarding program, including a CliftonStrengths Assessment, coaching sessions, Individual Mission Planning (more on this one later), and other onboarding conversations, including instilling a continuous learning and growth culture beginning on Day One.

Onboarding is important because it sets the stage for success, but onboarding is also important because it is one of 5 key steps that drive inclusion. True inclusion drives engagement and crew-munity, our word for teamwork on steroids. So, is a good leader one who really invests in what it takes to get someone first contributing right away and next, one who creates other leaders? Without a doubt, the answer is yes. If the leadership in your organization is not involved in onboarding, doesn't see it as an important part of their role, and delegates it to others, they are missing a true piece of leadership that pays dividends. Leaders are not just about what Gallup calls "Command," leaders are about setting others up for success, as well as many, many other things.

So, we have spent a bit of time on onboarding, known on a submarine as check-in. We have also talked about the leaders who are responsible for this experience, whether they are a leader of one or many. We have alluded to a 5-part system that drives inclusion once the pieces are in place and leaders own them, which drives engagement. Engagement on a submarine was not measured when I was a sailor, but I can say this without hesitation: it was the most engaged place I have ever been. Why is that important? Because engagement, among other things, improves productivity and reduces safety incidences. Do you think safety on a nuclear submarine is important? Hell yes.

There is a lot of information on our patent-pending model in our first book and on our website, thesubmarineway.com. This model drives inclusion and engagement, and we will briefly discuss it here.

> Leaders understand that leadership is a feeling, an attitude, and a responsibility, but leaders should also understand that there are tangible steps that they can take that contribute to the success and engagement of others.

These tangible steps are the model that leaders must know, that leads to inclusion, engagement, and builds other leaders. As we discuss building leaders throughout this book, we will frequently refer to the parts of the model; the **Methodology, System, and Process.** These are very specific things that a leader can do to drive better inclusion in his or her teams, leading to a more successful mission.

The Methodology - Strength-based, Inclusion-focused, and Mission-oriented

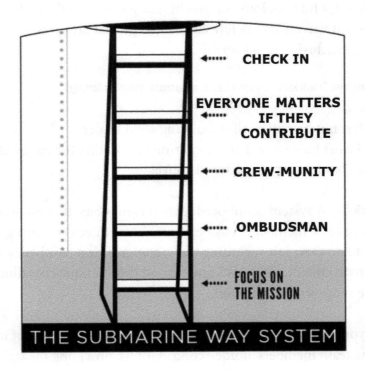

The System uses a methodology that recognizes and primarily focuses on what people are good at as an engine for better outcomes, what we call mission. While embracing what you are good at is important, it is also important to own what you are only OK at. It is important because when you do this, you know you need others to be successful.

> This drives inclusion, which we define as first being interdependent and then being collaborative.

Without these two critical pieces, without a focus on mission, results will be inconsistent. If every leader were to focus on this methodology, using this System to connect to people and assure their experience is good, leaders would be dealing with fewer issues caused by the backlash of poor leadership. Leadership is a little like inclusion, a bit nebulous because building leaders is the right thing to do, but there are very few tangible steps that are recommended to drive inclusion or leadership.

▍ There's an "I will know it when I see it" philosophy about leadership

which is not helpful at all in building solid leaders.

Here's how we at The Submarine Way define the rungs of the System ladder graphic pictured above:

Check-in: A system of onboarding that is so robust that upon completion, crew members (business associates) have everything they need to do their job, including tools, contacts, and familiarity with the environment. They also understand their unique contribution to the success of the mission.

Everyone Matters, if They Contribute: This is the process of identifying team members' unique contributions, providing the training to make sure they are successful, and then holding them accountable for results. (We use CliftonStrengths when we can, and train associates on their insight report.)

Crew-munity: This is a healthy team wherein individual strengths blend into a synergistic fighting machine, whether the fight is for revenue, client satisfaction, or fighting the bad guys at sea.

Choose an Ombudsman: An official liaison to the command, the ombudsman takes the pulse of the crew-munity. In the business world, the ombudsman has direct access to most senior leaders. These individuals must be able to drive change.

Focus on the Mission: This involves a clear understanding of the goals and core results needed for the organization and individuals. Do all employees, especially leaders, understand their contribution to the mission of the organization? You might be shocked at what you would hear if you were to ask.

Once the system is firmly in place and you as a leader are driving a better onboarding, seeing people through a strength-based lens, creating crew-munity, advocating for them and focusing them on the mission, you need a methodology and a process. These hold the System in place and anchor them to better results.

The last process that anchors the system and the methodology in place is CORE.

C—Commitment. Leaders need to be committed to the success of every individual in the command, company, or community. Leaders show their commitment in a variety of different ways, but to make sure the System is in place is a key step.

O—On-target training. On submarines, we drill and drill and drill. We also take professional development very seriously. If leaders are not committed to the growth of their people, engagement will be compromised. Millennials value learning and growth over latte bars and rock-climbing walls. In fact, professional development is important to every generation.

R—Reinforcement. Excellent training, if not reinforced, will succumb to learning decay. 90% of all training not reinforced will be forgotten in 30 days. That is why on submarines, we drill, drill, and drill some more. Not drilling? Train. Not training? Study.

E—Excellent results. If you follow the first three steps of CORE, you will get excellent results.

Once you understand the methodology, the System, and the process, you are ready to learn about the Five Anchors of Leadership. Obviously, good leadership takes a lot more than just developing these five characteristics, but if a leader were to focus on the methodology, the System, and the process, along with the Five Anchors of Leadership, leadership development itself would be instantly accelerated. As each chapter unfolds, the details of the Five Anchors of Leadership will be revealed. But first, here's a quick overview of the Five Anchors of Leadership before we take a deep dive into the following chapters that cover the anchors in detail.

The Five Anchors of Leadership

Anchor 1: Fighting the submarine takes a crew-munity. Leaders are collaborative and they encourage interdependency. They ask for input from their people and from all people where that input is value-added. This sets the stage for an inclusive leader.

Anchor 2: Captains are willing to go down with the ship. Leaders are accountable as leaders themselves and ready to go down if necessary, as they at the same time hold others accountable.

Anchor 3: Who is your sea daddy? Update: There are now sea mommies on submarines, and we welcome all those who coach and teach. Leaders value continuous professional development in themselves and insist on it for others. They read books on leadership and on their area of strength and don't assume they have reached a pinnacle of anything, where learning stops.

Anchor 4: Surface with your strengths or you will sink with your weaknesses. Leaders value what their people and others are good at.

They have a way of focusing on and developing strengths. For too long, managers saw performance reviews as a time reserved for telling people what they weren't good at. A strength-based leader manages areas of opportunity but helps their people excel and become pointy (near-perfect performance in an area). Becoming pointy, rather than well-rounded, means interdependence and collaboration are essential. This also sets a stage for inclusion to happen. Being pointy does not happen immediately. It's best to be a generalist until you learn where your talents lie and what talents need to be honed to a strength. Deb says that great careers are made by zigging and zagging; straight lines don't exist. I write more about this later.

Anchor 5: Crew-munity starts with the crew. Leaders have caring and concern about the people they lead. They want each person to feel valued and be engaged, and want the team to be better than its individual parts. Leaders are not afraid to show they care about each member of the team as an individual. They also care about the unit or team. Our motto for our company and to instill in our clients is, "all of us will always be better than one of us," but starting first with the individuals and then caring about the crew.

As a leader, you can do everything right. You can onboard, drive crew-munity, mentor, focus on the mission, and embody The Five Anchors, and still, it doesn't work. I have had more than a few of those. Leading is about effort, focus, and as we have said in this quick overview, methodology, system, and process, but without the talent to work with, the leader cannot be successful.

Sometimes Things or People Go Wrong

Bucky Williams was a first-tour sailor who struggled from Day One. He was onboarded (checked-in) like everyone else and assigned a sea daddy (crewmember assigned to assist and motivate new sailors who are studying for their qualifications), but Bucky always lagged. He eventually earned his dolphins, meaning he received his qualification in submarines, which is not easy and served as proof that he could meet the standards, but it took a huge commitment from just about everyone for him to get them. He struggled on watch, and specifically, his instincts and performance during emergency situations were not up to standards. As a result, at some point he would be dangerous to the crew or compromise the mission.

When I knew Bucky was not going to be successful, it was both my failure and his. We were practically family, and the crew—usually brutal if they thought the new sailor was lazy—loved Bucky and wanted him to be successful. When I recall this memory, it still stings. I could not recommend Bucky for retention at the end of his tour. In fact, for me to recommend Bucky for retention would be irresponsible. Leaders develop people, hold them accountable, and in the case of someone not having talent in any area critical to a role, they cut their losses. It stings; it's devastating to the person being cut, but that level of accountability is required.

Bucky went back to the Midwest, started farming, hosted a radio show, married, had children and a successful life. He said to me after it was all said and done, "Thanks for not recommending me for retention. It was the best thing to happen to me."

Hard to know at the moment, and not all stories like this end this way, but doing what's right almost always pays dividends.

Beyond the Five Anchors of Leadership, we talk about the responsibility of a leader when leading is not easy (chapter 8); we also talk about establishing a personal leadership creed and the importance of setting personal goals in chapter 9. We also talk about not setting personal goals and the impact of a ship operating rudderless, operating without navigation.

DEEP DIVE

ON CREATING BETTER LEADERSHIP IN YOU AND YOUR LEADERS

Questions to get you thinking:

1. When do you start investing in your new leaders? When they are identified as a high potential? Their first day? When they are promoted the first time?
2. Do you believe that everyone can lead, even if it is a subject matter expert?
3. Are leaders born or made?
4. How do the Methodology, System, and Process help leaders be better?
5. Are there other leadership qualities you believe are critical to a successful leader?

Three things to consider while navigating the Methodology, System, and Process:

1. Having an inclusive mindset as a leader will set you apart from other leaders.

2.   The System is so unique there is a patent pending on it.

3.   With many organizations, any investment in leadership is measured in ROI. Do you know how to measure the success of your leadership in terms of return on investment?

CHAPTER 2

ANCHOR 1: FIGHTING THE SUBMARINE TAKES A CREW-MUNITY

Leaders are Interdependent and Collaborative

Deb has always said she prefers to be nice as a leader; but given a choice between collaborative and effective, she'd rather be effective. Collaboration is critical. She says and demonstrates this as the president of our company, but when that fails, she's decisive, giving choices and following them through. Recently, a trusted vendor—who we were dependent on and that we had been in a contract with for a year—radically changed a business practice that would negatively affect us. Deb exchanged polite emails with the company, but they would not budge. Her next move clearly demonstrated the strong leader she is; she got them on the phone and told them they had one choice, revert to the model we signed up for or expect the business to be moved to another vendor. Clear about her determination, they reverted to the old model and they retained our business. Always try collaboration first but be prepared to move to what's most effective.

Living Interdependent, Collaborative Leadership

I was on the *L. Mendel Rivers* twice. In fact, nearly half of my fourteen years under the oceans were spent on this magnificent boat. My second tour was right after she came out of a major overhaul to convert her to the Navy's very first SDV (SEAL delivery vehicle) submarine. The concept was a small, semi-submersible that would be contained in a shelter, referred to as a dry deck shelter. Think of a luggage roof rack for a car, only large and heavy. This shelter would mount to the submarine's weapons shipping hatch and allow people—in this case, Navy SEALs, Explosive Ordinance Detail (EOD) personnel, and divers—to move between the submarine and the shelter and deploy. There was also piping connected to the submarine, allowing for filling the shelter with seawater and equalizing it with sea pressure. The outer door could be opened. The SDV could go out with the teams; the teams would conduct their missions and then return. The outer door would be closed, the shelter drained, and then the team could open the hatch connected to the submarine and return below. In theory, a pretty straightforward operation.

This operation was the very definition of interdependent collaboration utilizing different strengths to achieve the mission. Not everyone can be a SEAL or EOD specialist. That being said, they had not a clue in what was required to put a submarine in a launch posture. The third component that we needed was a common language or translators to communicate between SEALS and the team operating the submarine, which was a critical talent. One big hitch in the seemingly straightforward operation was that we were flooding this shelter with thousands of gallons of water while the submarine itself was almost motionless in the ocean. A submarine is designed to be able to control its buoyancy so that it is neither light (pops out of the water) nor sinks (you can figure out the problem there) when it is hovering or not moving through the water.

A submarine popping out of the water in an unexpected place could cause an international incident. Losing depth control and sinking endangers the submarine and its entire crew. BOTH will likely result in serious injury or death to those in the shelter.

Because of factors such as water temperature and how much food and liquids are in the tanks, a submarine uses seawater to fill other tanks to make the submarine heavier or pumps to get rid of this water to make the submarine lighter. The way a submarine stays on the surface is because these things called ballast tanks are full of air, making the submarine buoyant. When you want to submerge, you open the vents to the ballast tanks, water fills the ballast tanks, and the submarine submerges.

A lot of detail, I know, but why is this important? Because conducting a mission using the SEAL delivery vehicle was the most collaborative and interdependent activity a leader could participate in.

Failure to lead when necessary or back off when necessary could result in more than the failure of the mission; lives could be lost.

The officer of the deck is technically in charge of these operations, but the commanding officer is always present. A diving officer is responsible for maintaining the depth through orders to the helmsman, who uses planes, and to the chief of the watch, who uses pumps and flood valves to maintain depth. This is very challenging at slow speeds; near the surface, it is infinitely more challenging when tens of thousands of pounds of water were being flooded into a shelter.

When we started this initiative, this had never been done before, ever. We had theoretical tables and charts from the architects and "experts," all of which we abandoned within the first day of testing. We replaced the tables with notebooks and pens to record what was working, and, quite frankly, what wasn't working.

So, let the dance begin. Initial testing was done without any person in the chamber, just the control room team and the dry deck shelter officer, part of the SEAL team. Eventually, the shelter officer would be in constant contact with the SEALs and EOD personnel in the shelter directing how much the flood valves were open, as well as controlling the orders for opening and closing the door to the shelter and deployment and recovery of the SDV. This is "the dance": if flood water enters in too fast and the diving officer is not simultaneously pumping the same amount of water out of the auxiliary tanks, the submarine sinks; sometimes it really sinks, and you must increase speed and start all over. This can often take a long time and jeopardize the mission. If, on the other hand, the submarine pumps are removing water much faster than the valves in the dry deck shelter are allowing water in, the submarine gets light and, of course, this time losing depth control towards the surface and risking popping out of the water. So, do you see the symphony of leadership here? There's no room for ego, just a desire to make this mission work. This is collaboration and interdependency, utilizing expertise, and focus on the mission at its finest.

| There's also deep trust because everyone is pointy, which I will explain more about later.

Why is collaboration important to leadership? Hopefully, we gave you an example that was useful on submarines, but Deb was always known as an executive leader who built solid relationships with her peer groups in the business world, and as a result, she could tap into all kinds of talent all over the large Fortune 500 companies she worked for. If she had never programmed a voice recognition IVR (Interactive Voice Response), that was OK. She knew Miguel, who was excellent at it, and they made great partners in driving that project to completion. People wanted to help her and wanted to work with her. Given a choice between someone who wasn't a good partner, wasn't collaborative, and didn't want to be accountable, she was a great choice and didn't lack for colleagues. Then there were the people who worked for her. She had heart, head, and talent, and the success of her teams was very important to her. It was a winning combination, collaboration with peers and team, to drive better results.

In the Navy, specifically the submarine force, collaboration was necessary to get anything done. Leaders not only led their people but also had projects, including helping people qualify and leading missions; they were also career counselors. It was the best example of a role mentality, about which we will cover more later. The interdependent collaboration was such a part of the fabric of everything we did that, years later, I am still connected to so many of my old crew(s). Many of us are in the business world and we are still looking out for each other. A Navy colleague is a part of The Submarine Way today.

Interdependency is another critical component of making collaboration work. In fact, I say this in keynotes and workshops, go for interdependent first, then add collaboration. Interdependency drives better collaboration. Healthy interdependency is so important and so valuable that leaders can be pointy and be successful. Gone are the days of people who are successful because they are well rounded. Being pointy means they are very good at just a couple of things, what Gallup calls a strength, which becomes near-perfect performance. Being great at a couple of things means you need other people who are great at a whole set of different things, pointy in their areas. It is critical for a leader to be interdependent and encourage others to be interdependent.

> Leaning on each other, coaching, and helping each other drive inclusion and assures that "all of us are better than one of us." Leadership in the business world would benefit from more symphonies of leadership.

Too often, leadership is more about career climbing, being more visible for the same purpose, being right, or insecurity and not about the singular focus on the mission. What if meeting strategic goals was accomplished through a perfect symphony of all leaders who helped to contribute to the organization's goals? The conflict that affects productivity would be almost nonexistent. Many organizations have no problem coming up with too many annual goals they want to accomplish, but the reality is that only one or two get done because of internal issues and a lack of focus.

A Symphony of Leadership That is Strengths Based

A personal development mission is the culmination of talents and strengths, along with those things that bring joy pointed towards dreams of achievement in any area of life.

Another big collaborative event that clearly shows the symphony of leadership was a pier-side overhaul of a submarine. We stripped and recoated every steel deck, powder coated all the grates of the submarine, removed, repaired and replaced so many pieces of equipment I can't possibly remember or name them, then performed a complete electrical system overhaul, and that's just a snapshot of a month's worth of activity. Imagine your home being gutted with all the ventilation and electrical systems repaired or replaced. This was while the submarine was in the water, with the entire crew on shift work, 12 hours on and 12 off for a month. The point here is that I was the overall coordinator and I don't have a technical background. I know what an oxygen generator is and many of the necessary equipment needed for us to survive but had no idea exactly what needed to be done.

I was chosen because I was a good leader and an even better collaborator. I ended up touching every shift, every person, every expert, multiple times. Remember, I was not an expert. I had to collaborate and connect with multiple people to accomplish this effort in the necessary timeframe. Submarines are not meant to sit at the pier. Well, the project was completed; planning and collaboration allowed it to be done efficiently, tapping into what everyone was good at, and we met the timeframe. Without interdependent collaboration, this would have been a disaster. I was also pointy, which means I had very specific expertise in areas of leadership, but being pointy could mean you are an expert in another specific area.

Communication, interdependence, and leading were all strengths of mine, and those strengths often led to me leading a team to do something important outside a technical area of talent. This also serves as a great example of focusing first on the mission and then backing into who is best to fill what roles. In this case, it was going to take exacting coordination and people going beyond our high expectations to get this overhaul done on schedule. Due to the overwhelming technical nature of this operation, most organizations would choose someone with technical expertise. Often the person with technical expertise is not the best person to manage the project. They can be two very different skill sets. The submarine's focus on the needs of the mission allowed us to objectively identify the true expertise needed. The expertise needed was the ability to coordinate, collaborate, and frankly, be inspiring. Bottom line: respect and trust topped the list of required attributes.

One of our present clients is a city that faced a significant turnover of its most successful leaders through retirement. Its city manager, police chief, fire chief, and chief financial officer were all retiring within six months to twelve months of each other. This could be devastating to the operation of the city. The city manager, with foresight, asked us to come in and assess their high potential leaders two years before the departure of the critical senior leaders of this city. In addition to identifying these high potential leaders, we were going to develop them for their new roles. As this book unfolds, we will tell you more about how this turned out, but this leader was committed to collaborating for his city.

| He collaborated with his team, the mayor, the city council, and us.

He could have left the city in the hands of another city manager to figure out over time. That's the way most business is done, and he had given his thirty years already. That's not what he did. This city manager took a medium-sized city struggling with low growth because of the length of the "Great Recession" and compounded by the fact that much of the city's growth had ceded to suburban development trends. This resulted in disinvestment and blighting conditions within the downtown core and adjacent neighborhoods. At one point, there was also a racial divide; this city manager helped to transform the city so you could walk downtown after hours. He transformed the city into a place where any new business could open, recruit good people, and walk down the newly renovated downtown feeling safe and have fun. He was determined to leave it in this new, improved state, and in a position to grow and improve. He was successful because one of his strengths is his ability to collaborate towards a goal. More on this remarkable leader later.

On a submarine, collaboration is critical. Typically, on a rotation of port and starboard, you are on watch for 12 hours and off watch for 12 hours. Collaborating with the shift before and the shift after you means the submarine operates as it should, safely and with someone always being on watch and aware of any issues from shift to shift. So, does the average submariner see this as leadership? Some do; some don't. But you can bet that on most shifts, someone is leading the way to communicate, keep the boat safe and connect all of the pieces from shift to shift while someone else sleeps. It's why being qualified for watch duty is so important. We will talk a lot about collaborating toward a goal, or mission in this book, but what's the mission here? Getting the submarine safely to its mission, which in fact might be fighting the submarine.

Who's on watch in your organization, collaborating in case you must fight your submarine?

We work a lot with healthcare companies, and most frequently, hospitals that have a similar challenge with how to handle shifts. They also have a critical mission: the health and the safety of every patient. This takes communication between shifts, awareness of potential issues, and leadership skills from doctors to nurses, even assistants and janitorial staff to ensure every shift is providing care to the patient. The only thing at risk here is the health or life of the patient. Sound like an important challenge to you? Yet they accomplish it day after day. When done well, it looks easy. A piece of this success, just like with submarines, is the interdependency of each healthcare professional providing care. They share information, concerns, and potential safety issues, so there is continuity of care for each patient. Hopefully, you noticed we included janitorial staff when talking about communication, leadership, and collaboration. If they do not do their job well regardless of how well everyone else does theirs, there will eventually be a serious problem. Treat them with the same respect you treat others. They deserve it.

Collaboration so far has been about coordinating and communicating between multiple shifts all involved in a common mission, or a mission like with the SDVs where all team members were working on a common goal at the same point in time, with leaders setting clear expectations about the criticality of collaboration and interdependency. The reality is that most modern workplaces are social and collaborative places on a daily basis. Millennials see the workplace as very social and very collaborative, and when it is not, they lose interest quickly. New or upcoming leaders should embrace this more readily than previous generations, although there will be exceptions.

> In many modern workplaces, collaboration is the engine of innovation.

Without a leader willing to embrace collaboration and innovation, the U.S. would fall behind more innovative countries. Today's leaders must be interdependent and collaborative or lead their companies down a path that will shorten the company's success. So how does a leader encourage collaboration as part of a workgroup? It can be difficult when the group is large to capture all the ideas, filter through them, and determine which ideas to move forward with. There are several software tools on the market that can help with collecting and distributing these innovative ideas. Without collaboration and without diversity of ideas, your organization is likely stuck in the past.

Leaders Have a Sense of Humor

> I love the expression, "Learn to laugh at yourself for a lifetime of free entertainment."

I don't know who coined that phrase, but that's where humor should be used, at one's self or at the situation. It should never be directed at someone else. Yes, we broke that rule on subs. There were, however, places we would not go. Girlfriends were fair game, and I made more than a few guys nervous when I went there. I was putting lotion on my face and body years ago, long before the line of men's products became popular. When I stepped out of the shower and took time to lather up with lotion, I was ruthlessly teased. The only way to survive that onslaught was to hit back hard. Usually, it took the form of telling the sailor in question that I put lotion on my skin because his girlfriend liked my skin smooth. So, way out of bounds in the business world, but on a sub, the offending sailor would immediately go quiet and I would never hear anything about putting lotion on again. Humor on the boats took all kinds of turns, but one thing we knew: humor was important to relieving stress. It's equally true in the business world. When I do keynotes, I always poke fun at myself. It's a fine line between poking a bit of fun and demeaning myself, so I'm careful to humanize without demeaning. Every leader should be able to use humor in a way that's effective for bonding and relieving stress. If that's not your thing, a strength-based mindset suggests having someone that can utilize humor on the team to help the team in bonding and stress relief.

The best way to remember the importance of interdependence and collaboration is through the following acronym: LEAD.

L—Learn to trust in the talents of others

E—Effectively utilize your own and others pointy strengths

A—Aim at the mission through a symphony of leadership

D—Determination through obstacles to utilize the team and accomplish the mission

Most leadership books have their version of the principles of leadership. Most are necessary, and if you focus on one system versus another, and focus on being a better leader, you won't go wrong. There is not just one formula to be a better leader. What about diversity? Should that be important to a leader? We talk a lot about inclusion in this book, and the value of leaders who embrace and drive inclusion through the System, the methodology and process, as well as good leadership. So, what role does diversity play in the life of a leader? We've implied that whether someone is female, gay, or African American is irrelevant to what they can accomplish. What makes our Five Anchors of Leadership different is that we are firmly committed to the criticality of diversity and the value of inclusion, as more than being the right thing to do, which they absolutely are. They are also, in fact, the most powerful driver of human behavioral change and, therefore, a superb business strategy. You won't read that anywhere else.

> If you are not a leader who sees the value of diverse ideas, of people, or gender, ethnicity, and truly care for the people you lead, you are limiting your potential as a leader.

Hard. Stop.

DEEP DIVE

INTO COLLABORATION AND INTERDEPENDENCE

A few questions to get you thinking and help you assess your operation:

1. Do you have a good sense of the talents and strengths your leaders have?
2. Do you think about your leaders as a perfect symphony to accomplish the mission, stepping in and out as their part is needed?
3. Do you expect your team members or leaders to collaborate towards a goal/mission? How are you making this clear to them?
4. What collaboration time are you providing your team to allow and encourage innovation?

Three things to help you navigate collaboration and interdependence:

1. These two characteristics create the start of inclusive environments.

2. Inclusive environments drive engagement and engagement drives ROI.

3. Leaders don't always head up organizations; they lead projects geared toward a variety of different outcomes and they are influencers. Without them, the result would be questionable.

CHAPTER 3

ANCHOR 2: CAPTAINS ARE WILLING TO GO DOWN WITH THE SHIP

Leaders are accountable as leaders, but they also hold others accountable

> Behavior that adversely affects the individual's performance, the team's performance, or the organization's performance must be addressed.

Period, hard stop. On submarines, we had something called a delinquent list. No, not that kind of delinquent. This was a list of things a sailor did not do timely like qualify for submarines or watch. For example, if you are not qualified for watch on a timely basis, others are doing your job, getting less sleep, and potentially putting the submarine at risk. If you are not qualified for submarines, if there's a casualty on board, fighting the submarine could be at risk.

Everything is for a reason; generally, it's about completing the mission, and safety is a huge part of that, and there is a great deal of pressure to get people back on track quickly. Almost 90% of sailors qualify for submarines and go on to serve multiple years. The process for holding others accountable is clear, with clear roles, including mid-level peers holding each other accountable, and it extends to that junior personnel as well. Everyone is responsible for accountability. What are the critical elements in your organization that are like fighting the submarine that you must hold others accountable for? Identify the must-haves and be prepared to address those issues immediately. Remember, everyone matters if they contribute; this is a critical part of the System, and discussed in *Diversity and Inclusion The Submarine Way* at length. To make sure everyone is contributing, accountability is critical.

Deb recalls one of the most difficult discussions she has ever had with an employee. She had received an email from a client that this employee, a Client Services Director, had missed a couple of critical deliverables. A budget that was due two weeks before, a white paper, and a presentation to the client had all slipped by their deadlines. Deb had a large operation with several directors, so trusting them to reach out if there were issues was very standard practice, and autonomy allowed the directors to operate with creativity and contributed to the harmony and client focus of the team. What made this a particularly sensitive issue was that the Director had been ill, and therefore had been in and out of the office. Deb had asked several times if there were issues with meeting deadlines and offered help, but the Director said she was fine and was meeting deadlines.

> When it was time to have the conversation with this Director, the Director knew she was not meeting deadlines, that it was likely the client had complained and that this was an accountability discussion, her defenses were up, and she was ready to fight.

Deb laid out the issue, using notes from her email and conversation with the client. The Director immediately got mad, arguing that no specific dates had been set, so she, therefore, was not late meeting deadlines. When Deb calmly said this was not the client's understanding of the situation, the Director began to cry. Her sobs filled the room. When they had abated, Deb suggested they meet again after the Director was calmer, and they find a way first to get the client what they needed, then address why the deadlines slipped—Deb was more than willing to help, and had offered this help. The second conversation went much better, but there are a couple of critical takeaways from the first discussion:

1. Accountability discussions cannot happen when either party is not calm. Delay the discussion until it can take place when the individual(s) is/are calmer.
2. Don't avoid having the discussion just because it will be a tough conversation. It won't get better with time.
3. Stay focused on the goal of the conversation. In this case, it was to get the client what they needed and had been promised.
4. You will need the input of the individual to figure out how to keep the same thing from happening again. Use collaboration skills to get this person to open up and determine how to get things back on track.

The need for having accountability discussions is obvious, but way too often, they never take place. We will talk about that later, but what about the importance of personal accountability?

How do you feel about leaders who hold you to a different standard than they hold themselves?

It can be quite frustrating. Until you are completely willing to accept that you are responsible for your thoughts, emotions, and actions, it is very hard to gain the respect of others and hold others accountable. If you aren't mission-focused, how can the team be? If your performance isn't the best it can be, how can you expect that of others? This is probably the biggest contradiction in many institutional leaders who then wonder why they have issues with people, constituents, or colleagues. Politicians expect us to live honest lives, pay our taxes, and stay out of debt while they are often not honest or frugal. It drives a wedge between leaders and those they lead every time there is a contradiction. Perfection isn't required, but what you say and what you do must be mostly aligned. Again, how do you feel when leaders' values are not aligned with their actions? When leaders are accountable for their actions and the outcomes of their decisions in all situations where they are involved, they do not blame others when things go in a way that is not planned. They pull the team together and determine what went wrong, even if that means they are responsible for miscommunication, or other issues affecting the outcome.

Once you have looked in the mirror and you know you are disciplined, that you are accountable, and looking through the lens of inclusion and strengths, you are ready to hold others accountable. Self-development is a lifelong effort so don't wait until you are perfect, you might never have that critical conversation, and believe that when people do not achieve the goal, they are really doing their best. If you approach it from any other standpoint, you are not approaching it in a way that will change behavior, and the recipient is likely to be defensive.

Building crew-munity and achieving the mission includes dealing with those who do not buy into the mission and are disruptive. Whatever the reason for this disruption, it needs to be addressed, or the mission is in jeopardy. Every piece of leadership learning, every discussion on accountability serves to return the focus to the mission after there's been a disruption, or to prepare when there's a new mission. Having these discussions on accountability is critical; otherwise, team members will not perform as you'd expect and achieve the mission.

A Young Sailor (Me) Makes a Big Mistake

Early in my career, I had a very unfortunate accountability discussion with a seaman. I was a very junior leader who had a very high standard for myself and others. I worked hard and hardly slept, which brought out an edgy quality that I am not all that proud of. This particular seaman worked hard, very hard, but he just could not be successful. Everyone knew it, almost from the very beginning, and it was not getting better with time. One day, out of complete frustration at something he did, completely unplanned, I started yelling at him. We were in port for the next few days, so I told him to get off the boat. By the way, he was in the duty section and not allowed the leave the boat. I knew this, disregarded it, and pushed forward. I used colorful sailor language—they don't say swore like a sailor for nothing—and in front of everyone, I berated him. I still cringe at what I said. Well, after I yelled at him, we parted company, and never did I imagine he would leave the boat but leave he did.

> We were both in trouble, but since I told him to leave and was his senior, I was significantly more responsible.

When I became aware that he'd left, I went topside and to the pier and brought him back. I took full responsibility, telling my duty officer and navigator what I had done. I told them he was not responsible for leaving the boat, that he did that at my direction, my order, unlawful as it was. I never lost my temper quite like that again. I learned to walk away when I knew my emotions were high, most of the time. I also doubled down my efforts with this seaman. I equaled his commitment, and he increased his, and eventually, he became competent. It doesn't always have a happy ending, but this time it did.

So, what lessons did I learn from that situation? Just like I said earlier, if either party is emotional, the outcome is going to be questionable. I also did not assume he was doing his best, and I should have. In retrospect, I think he was trying; but when I increased my efforts and gave him clearer and calmer suggestions, we both rose to the occasion. He was never going to be a superstar, but he was reliable, competent, and that makes all the difference. When your reaction to an accountability discussion is emotional, it will almost always reduce motivation. I had two problems after this situation, his reaction and emotion, which was as close to being demotivated as it could be, and my situation, I was in trouble with my leadership over my overreaction. Once I tackled both issues, I apologized to this seaman and the leaders I reported to. I still needed to solve the problem that got me to this place.

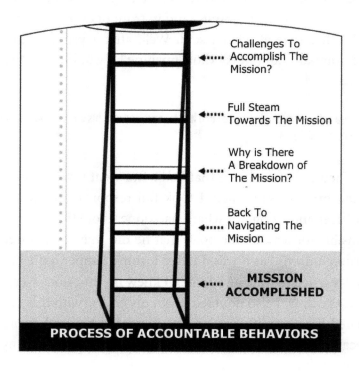

Challenges To Accomplish The Mission?

Full Steam Towards The Mission

Why is There A Breakdown of The Mission?

Back To Navigating The Mission

MISSION ACCOMPLISHED

PROCESS OF ACCOUNTABLE BEHAVIORS

Solving the problem should always start with discovering "why." Deb's experience with LEAN taught her the importance of the 5 Whys root cause technique. Start first by asking why you got the result you did. In this case, I needed to ask this seaman what he thought was contributing to his lack of success. And when I got this answer, I asked why again. Each why asked after each answer contributes to a deeper understanding of the root cause. My actual unraveling of the why was a much slower process, but eventually I got there and we solved the issues together.

The submarine ladder model is a fitting way to model accountable behaviors

Remember, the submarine model is always inverted. You never go up the ladder, but always down. If this is a long mission, you may be checking in or moving up and down the ladder with multiple people and multiple scenarios. You might be holding someone accountable for not qualifying for a watch, while you are holding someone else accountable for an assignment related to fighting the submarine.

For our healthcare friends, in a hospital system, the same situation. Someone might be late for a shift and thus the need for an accountability discussion, while progress is being monitored for a patient and a discussion happening because someone hasn't completed their continuing education. Having these discussions doesn't have to be time consuming but can head off obstacles to the mission before there's a complete setback. This is not just applicable to healthcare, although I discussed this specifically because they also use high reliability as a tool, but any business can utilize the lowest accountability to get the job done. When everyone leads, regardless of age or title, the business wins.

The bottom line: don't avoid these discussions. Done correctly, they keep the submarine on course.

Emotional Intelligence and the Leadership Partnership

Deb and I agree on the importance of emotional intelligence in an individual in order for them to be successful as a leader, but we disagree on whether this is an innate talent that builds to a strength or a skill that can be learned.

> Deb's position is that emotional intelligence is a talent like any other, and if that talent doesn't exist in that individual, you can't teach it.

I believe that, based on other talents like communication, command, or strategy, emotional intelligence can become a skill developed from other talents. Regardless of whether it is a talent or a skill that develops over time, we agree that it is necessary for the success of a leader to have it.

So, what is emotional intelligence? Emotional intelligence is generally understood as the ability to understand one's own emotions, to identify them before they are an issue in the situation, or to identify them to leverage them in a situation. It is also an awareness of other people's emotions for the same purpose. In fact, I would argue that a major component of accountability is emotional intelligence. If my emotions rule my thought process, including my ego, I am likely not making decisions that are logical, objective, or will obtain the best outcome of the situation.

> Learning to manage my emotions and understand another's will give me an advantage in situations that others might be blinded by.

Four tips for improving emotional intelligence:

1. When appropriate, practice adapting to a new norm, standard, or goal. Manage your reaction to the change and help others to adapt to the change. Growth is inevitable.
2. If your inclination is to get upset or go negative in certain situations, identify this upfront. When you find yourself in one of these situations, stay calm, use the reason you already developed for these situations, and immediately apply it. Learn to identify these same flashpoints in your key players and help them with managing the situation in a similar way.
3. Harness the power of emotion by learning to identify positive and negative emotions in one on one and group settings. Decide in advance strategies for managing the situation. Remain calm and implement your plan. Like all practice, it becomes muscle memory.
4. Practice hearing the personal situations, including feelings of individuals within the team. Learning to really listen, while managing your emotions will build emotional intelligence skills.

DEEP DIVE

INTO ACCOUNTABILITY FOR BOTH THE CAPTAIN AND THE CREW

Questions to get you thinking:

1. Do you believe your integrity as a leader is important? How do you demonstrate it?
2. Even if the conversations are difficult, do you hold accountability discussions before the issues become obstacles?
3. If there is a problem, how do you get the mission back on track?

Two ways to navigate accountability:

1. Delaying tough discussions doesn't get better with time. Have these discussions in a timely manner.
2. Do not continue a discussion when you or the receiver is emotional. Both the message giver and the receiver will have difficulty with the message.

CHAPTER 4

ANCHOR 3: WHO IS YOUR SEA DADDY?

Leaders Believe in Continuous Professional Development

A sea daddy is a role almost everyone on a submarine plays at some point in time. With women now serving on submarines for over a decade now, there are some sea mommies as well. With 110 people on board, everyone was responsible for everything. Being Assistant Navigator and a diving officer were my primary jobs, but submarine comedian, sea daddy, and a career development chief were additional roles.

> As we've learned about the symphony of leadership, roles done well are a symphony.

Anyone who can move from role to role seamlessly is leading, even if they are primarily a subject matter expert. A Sea Daddy as a role is responsible for the qualification of new sailors. They take this job very seriously, sometimes because they are expected to, or they are naturally leading the way, and sometimes it's simply because the more people qualified for a watch, the better. Whatever the motive, the role of sea daddy is very important.

Continuous professional development can take many forms. Leadership stories do not always have to be inspiring to be effective; sometimes, fear can shake things up. I was a brand-new crew member on my very first submarine when my unique leadership story happened. As I said, I had extensive navigational knowledge and had finished at the top of both my Quartermaster (think navigation) school and submarine school. I was going to show up and take off! I was made for this, and everyone would recognize it right away. Well, not so much. I was certainly going to get qualified for in-port watch station, but underway, I was not going to be navigating, I was going to be washing dishes, scrubbing toilets and compacting trash. Why? Well, that is where I was going to be most helpful, that's why. I caught a break though—sad for them, good for me—because two qualified quartermasters in a five-person division got popped on a drug screening, disqualifying them from submarines, meaning they were gone. I would like to think I felt bad for them, although I have no such recollection. Without enough time to get replacements, my value now shifted to the quartermaster division. Don't get me wrong; my day job remained dishes and toilets, but my new task was to begin the extensive qualification process to become qualified to navigate a nuclear submarine underway. It is very important to note that there are no corners cut in submarine qualifications or watch qualifications. There is no such thing as teaching them the basics, and we'll get to the rest later. Nope; you demonstrate, in detail, your ability to handle decisions and the required knowledge to make those decisions, or you do not get qualified. Period. Hard stop.

Professional Development the Cowboy Jim Way

I did what I could in port, but it was while underway where I essentially spent all my time—after scrubbing dishes and toilets—learning submarines and learning the watch station. Since I had such a strong navigation background from my schooling at SUNY Maritime and my Merchant Marine service, I knew navigation but not submarine navigation. Submarine navigation in the early 1980s was as much instinct and art as it was science. I had the instincts; I quickly learned the science and procedures. After a very brief time, I got all the way through the qualifications and was taken away from full-time dishwashing and toilet cleaning (the toilet cleaning now was just a part-time job), and I began standing watch. The person in charge of the division was a crusty, mean, old-school senior chief, who was brutal on me during my qualifications and worse once I was qualified.

Let's just get this out of the way. I was cocky, really cocky.

I knew I was good, just not as good as I thought I was, and Cowboy Jim (our nickname for the senior chief, earned from his upbringing in the southwest, riding rodeo bulls for fun, prior to entering the Navy) had his stink eye on me every minute. He would consistently point out my breaks from the procedure that I viewed as important innovations. He saw it as "not doing what the hell he was telling me to do," and it was unacceptable. This dance went on for weeks. I would do something a bit differently; he would very directly correct me. I would comply for a bit and then either start again or go to another area with another better way to do it.

One day, Cowboy Jim reached his breaking point. I don't remember what my latest innovation was, but boy, do I remember his reaction. He exploded, literally, full color in his language and in the purple veins bulging from his neck and forehead. In front of about six other watch standers, he completely verbally obliterated me. When he was done (about two minutes of fury), I replied with the following: "You would not be talking so much shit if you did not have those anchors on your collar." (The chief's insignia is a fouled anchor and Cowboy Jim always wore the actual metal ones rather than the sewn-on variety popular with most submariners.) In that next second, he rebutted me with a crazed look—and I mean crazed in a way I have never been looked at—and said, "Follow me." Understand, as the quartermaster (navigator) on watch, I was not allowed to leave my station for even a minute without the express permission of the officer of the deck, but leave I did, and the officer of the deck said not a word.

I followed Cowboy down the passageway, forward to an electronics space, just beyond the Commanding Officer's stateroom and adjacent to the Executive Officer's (the #2-most senior person on a submarine). The CO was not in his stateroom, but the executive officer was. I proceeded to that electronics space, and Cowboy Jim paused and literally said to the executive officer in a voice plainly audible to me: "You need to take a walk, sir." The XO did just that. Cowboy Jim came in the electronics space, almost slammed the door, and got about three inches from my face.

> His eyes full of rage, purple veins more pronounced than ever, and his face had turned to a fire engine red.

In one motion, he reached up with both his hands, grabbing and ripping off both his anchors from his collar. Immediately dropping his now-clenched fists into a clear fighting stance, he said, "I ain't wearing anchors now, you little m----&%#@!!! I literally still remember the clanking sound the anchors made as they fell between the deck and the hull, coming to rest somewhere in the bowels of the compartment, never to be seen again.

I realized he was, at a minimum, going to beat me up and who knew what else, and I was terrified. My expertise in using my fists in anger had resulted in a lifetime record of 0-20. I was much better verbally, although my mouth got me into trouble as many times as it got me out of trouble, as evidenced by the situation I got myself in with Cowboy. Good verbal skills and light on my feet tended to be entertaining and funny, but, in this case, not good for my safety. I immediately backed down and moved away from him. I apologized for causing the situation and assured Cowboy Jim I would never do anything other than what he said, and the procedures dictated. You know what? I never did. Leadership like this is an interesting example, but this is much more sophisticated than is obvious. On a submarine, the mission is everything, and anything that risks the mission (watchstanders who ignore time-tested procedures is a great example) cannot be tolerated.

Cowboy Jim did not possess the nurturing feedback gene. What he did possess was a unique talent to figure out how to communicate effectively to everyone he engaged with. What I mean by that is, what I saw as him picking on me initially, was his understanding that I was very talented, very brash, and would always be pushing the envelope. I later noticed he never spent any time around other watchstanders. I also never saw him have direct conversations with others over the coming months that ever came anywhere near what he did with me. At the end of the day, I am not advocating for violence and threats, but by God, he found the only way to get me to do what I should have been doing. Literally nothing is more important than the safe navigation of this submarine, and Cowboy Jim was not interested in rolling the dice.

There were great lessons learned at that moment in the electronics space. I also, after that day, always wore "hardware" (metal instead of cloth insignias) for my entire submarine career. I realized different people require different approaches and styles, and most importantly, accountability to one's self and the continuous development of others is critical but never at the sacrifice of mission focus. Cowboy, despite my best efforts to undermine him and me, was committed to developing this talented, if stubborn, new sailor. I was never the same after that, and that was a good thing.

So, if you have read any of the popular Naval leadership books, there are two types of leaders: those expecting to be and some becoming demi-gods, valuing being right and being in charge over being effective, and then others who are truly innovative leaders that encourage innovation and self-development in others. Cowboy Jim was a chief petty officer, not a captain, and he was not simply trying to be right but to push my self-development; innovation, not so much.

> **This book is about the importance of leadership at all levels.**

Although certainly an extreme example, Cowboy Jim knew I needed a direct approach. I am not in any way saying this is the right approach, but if someone needs guidance and they require a more direct conversation, channel Cowboy Jim and add a few filters. Never forget that the mission cannot be compromised. If accountability means some tough love or means someone needs to leave the boat, make your decision and stick by it.

In Gallup's article, "State of the American Manager," they talk about grow, don't promote, stating that many companies put people in leadership positions because they were good at their last role or because of tenure. A tenure-based or strictly performance-based decision to choose leaders will ultimately fail. Leaders should be chosen because of talent, developed and coached because from that talent they can develop strengths. Gearing the feedback and the type of professional development—in this case, I needed direct, in-my-face feedback—will be effective if the other person is willing to develop. As tough as my conversation was with Cowboy Jim, it was a very personal message that I didn't fail to understand. Over time, it was clear that Cowboy Jim saw my talent and strengths and was helping me to develop in the way I needed.

Another recent Gallup study indicated that 55% of millennials value learning and growing beyond anything else. Current thinking about millennials is that they value latte bars and rock-climbing walls. Well, they might, but even if you have these, you will not find millennials willing to stay at your organization and contribute to the degree they are capable if there isn't an investment in their professional development. This kind of investment does pay it forward. Choose a strength-based leader, put an individual mission plan in place (IMP), a plan the leader and individual co-own, make sure they get what they need to grow—training, feedback, coaching—and you will find that leader pays it forward with the people they develop as well.

The client I talked about earlier (city in South Carolina) asked us to identify high potentials to become new leaders in the city. These leaders would backfill roles vacated by the leaders who planned on retiring soon. As you would expect, a half-dozen departures at senior levels would cause a ripple effect throughout the organization. To identify and classify the high potential talent in this city, we used a modified 9 Box. 9 Box is a tool that allows leaders to put talent into one of nine boxes that describe potential from the standpoint of current performance and future potential. We call this a modified 9 Box because the program we developed looks at talent not only in terms of current performance, but potential based on talents and strengths. Over 35 individuals were identified based on this criterion as high potential candidates; another 30 were identified as emerging leaders. What do we mean by talents and strengths? We asked the current leaders to assess potential talent in terms of talent pools. We will take a deep dive into this in the chapter on strengths, but we asked these leaders to have a vision about the future of the city, to look beyond gender, ethnicity, and any other criteria other than talent and strengths.

Once these 65 individuals were identified, we put together a professional development program for the high potentials and the emerging leaders. The high potentials have completed the curriculum and are doing reinforcement. Remember, reinforcement is critical. Without it, there's a 90% learning decay after 30 days. Well, this group has become infused with an inclusive mission focus, is changing the way they do onboarding, and leads with a strength-based mindset. The future of this organization is bright, and we will watch with anticipation as these new leaders begin to fill vacancies and make their mark on the future.

We have hundreds of conversations with employers annually about professional development for their people. We help them to discover their unique return on investment. Is it reducing turnover? Is it improving safety in high-tech manufacturing or a healthcare setting? Those clients we get to really think about the value of professional development through ROI are willing to make the commitment and see the benefit because they see it through.

To invest and train your leaders is a gift that keeps on giving. These leaders coach, model, and require good performance from the people they develop to be leaders. Professionally develop your leaders early because bad habits, or worse, apathy, sets in quickly.

> **Spend most of your time developing your best, not in trying to build up your average performers.**

One other bit of advice for you: make sure to encourage your leaders to read. If you can't afford anything else because of budget constraints, buy key leaders a book on leadership twice a year, and have these books discussed in team meetings so everyone can benefit. Investing in your best, those people who are influencers, is smart business.

> **And for all you leaders seeking continuous professional development for yourselves, if you are not constantly reading, writing, or learning about leadership, you will lose your edge.**

Set aside time for it; plan the two or three conferences that can help keep you sharp; choose the top two or three books that will help you learn something new about leadership, and share this with others. If your organization doesn't invest in you, invest in yourself. You don't need anyone's permission to develop personally and professionally.

In 2019, we decided to add personal development to all our efforts. Our objective had always been to help communities, organizations, and universities, but it became increasingly obvious that individuals were looking for ways to grow beyond what their organizations were willing to do. There are several good solutions out there for the individual, in addition to ours. We added training videos, the Gallup CliftonStrengths assessment, and our unique view of the insight report to our offerings. We have been told that the Individual Mission Plan (IMP), our proprietary plan to help the individual develop specific steps towards personal change and personal development, has helped people plan positive changes in their lives. Keeping the light on for leadership is a lifelong quest.

Professional Development on a T Boat

After being assigned my first shore duty as the submarine exercise area coordinator (think an air traffic controller of submarines), in Charleston, South Carolina, I very quickly realized that being anything but the tip of the spear was boring, if not almost intolerable. I immediately started looking for something else to keep me stimulated, and while driving one day, I saw a huge boat sitting in a cradle next to the Cooper River in a remote area of the Navy base. She was 90 feet long, steel, and clearly older. Of course, I stopped and had to check this boat out. When I climbed on board her, there were chart tables, a conning station, and the wheelhouse had a wooden helm and brass everywhere. Below in the engine room was a massive Caterpillar diesel engine. I found out later it was the original diesel engine. I did some research and found out this was a T boat and was originally built during World War II to deliver cargo on the Intracoastal Waterways. The Intracoastal Waterways were envisioned as early as 1808 by Treasurer Gallatin and we realized the importance of its development during the War of 1812. They became critical during WWII to safely move cargo while avoiding German submarines patrolling off our coast, picking off ships carrying cargo. For some reason, after the war, this thing ended up at the Naval Weapons Station. It had been modified for something.

Well, this bored, bright, brand-new Chief Petty Officer began to think about ways to use this big, beautiful boat.

There were great multi-million-dollar navigation simulators for trainees back then, and I'm sure even more impressive ones now exist. They would simulate going upriver. They could make it look foggy or bright, so a fantastic virtual training resource.

Nothing is as cool as the wind in your face and having a man overboard drill outside on the water, however, and I had decided that this boat would be perfect for on-the-job training.

I developed tables to do advance and transfer so this ship would act and turn at the rate a submarine would. The boat was surveyed and found sound. I convinced the admiral of submarine group six we should have a training group on this ship, and, much to my surprise, the answer was yes. We moved the boat to a pier, and I began to select those junior enlisted getting thrown out of the Navy to be my crew. It was a bit like *McHale's Navy*. The show might be a bit dated, but it was a perfect description of my crew. By the way, I was not a senior person. I was a brand-new Chief Petty Officer with seven years of service. I was motivated to be a leader, and I wanted to build other leaders, and professional training is a key element. Eventually, I wanted to add surface ships.

There was only one big problem. I had to be qualified as Craftmaster of this boat, named the *Donald P Hall*, that big, beautiful World War II cargo boat. Almost no submariner ever qualifies Craftmaster and there was not anyone to train me at the submarine group. I had to qualify with a bunch of crusty boatswain's mates, on tugboats, who put me through hell to get it done. It was hazing and brutality Part II. To them, a submariner was not worthy of this endeavor. I looked very young, always cocky, and they just did not like me. Impossible to break, I eventually got qualified, got my crew trained, and went to work marketing and advertising "live navigation training." Let's just say business was slow, and the submarine group was growing impatient with my "big idea." I was determined to make my mark when my big break came.

I was buying a beer out of a machine on base for lunch one day, yes, beer machines in the barracks—man, I loved the Navy. I noticed a large group of what I thought were ROTC students (think college kids in Navy uniforms.) These turned out to be midshipmen from the Naval Academy. They looked bored, and well, they looked bored. I started chatting with them and their officer in charge, a young lieutenant, and discovered that their plans for getting underway on a destroyer for two weeks had been canceled, and they had nowhere to go. I invited them on board and improvised navigation, man-overboard training, and a bunch of necessary training all out to sea on the *Donald P Hall*. For two weeks, I taught these young men and women more about piloting and navigation than they would have learned in a semester of school or during those two weeks on any type of Navy vessel. Although they went on to get underway on a Navy ship and did some other cool training, every one of them listed their time training on the *Donald P. Hall* as the best training they received all summer. Of course, this confused the coordinators at the Naval Academy because nobody there knew what the hell the *Donald P. Hall* was. Long story shortened, they found us, word spread, and soon I had more trainees then I could handle, adding surface ships and VIP tours for senior officers and politicians along the way. We became a training platform with a waiting list, crewed by young sailors awaiting discharge for everything from going AWOL (absent without leave) and drug use. We did have an amazing engineman and boatswain on loan from the submarine tender and eventually became a hot ticket.

There's a bunch of stories about leadership, perseverance, and ingenuity that hopefully can inspire readers to do more with less or to create opportunities where others see none. We didn't have air conditioning or heat on board before I started, much needed to be repaired, and I needed to sell this concept everywhere, enlisting the reporter of the Naval Base Charleston newspaper to write articles about us but let me summarize the important takeaways; but first, in the business world, you don't always get what you need or even what you want. You are understaffed and under-resourced. Learning to utilize every tool, including creativity, can help you make the most of every situation.

1. My *McHale's Navy* crew had a good parting experience from the Navy. I owe them a lot and appreciate that they were committed to making this work. To my engineman, Smokey, you made her sing. Thank you!

2. I wanted to excel, to give a maximum contribution and I stretched myself and my authority to get there.

3. Results matter and the feedback and result were beyond anything that was being done up to that point. They continued the program long after I left.

4. My professional development and the commitment to development the Navy had, as well as the sailors, played a significant role in this great experience and great training.

5. Deb often says you need to zig before you zag in building your career or helping others. Finally taking a break from sea duty after seven operational years was a zig. Creating my own training command was a zag—both were necessary.

DEEP DIVE

INTO PROFESSIONAL DEVELOPMENT

Questions to get you thinking:

1. Do you make investments in developing your leadership and in others as well?
2. Do you know any of the top two or three books on leadership that are published annually?
3. Do you know how to calculate the ROI of professional development?

Three things that help you navigate professional development:

1. Invest in your best people and expect them to pay it forward.
2. Set aside time to learn and grow and expect it of others.
3. Make sure millennials, and every generation, know and are part of creating their individual mission plans.

US 20200111045A1

(19) **United States**
(12) **Patent Application Publication** (10) Pub. No.: US 2020/0111045 A1
Fortin et al. (43) Pub. Date: **Apr. 9, 2020**

(54) **METHOD FOR ORGANIZING AND CARRYING OUT A TRAINING PROCESS**

(71) Applicant: **The Genesis Group LLC**, Bostic, NC (US)

(72) Inventors: **Deborah Cake Fortin**, Bostic, NC (US); **John Gregory Vincent**, Bostic, NC (US)

(21) Appl. No.: **16/153,851**

(22) Filed: **Oct. 8, 2018**

Publication Classification

(51) Int. Cl.
G06Q 10/06 (2006.01)
G09B 19/16 (2006.01)
(52) U.S. Cl.
CPC . *G06Q 10/063114* (2013.01); *G06Q 10/0637* (2013.01); *G06Q 10/06398* (2013.01); *G09B 19/162* (2013.01)

(57) **ABSTRACT**

A method is presented for organizing and carrying out a training program, a seminar or a workshop having a plurality of participants to assist each participant in improving an efficiency and function of a business organization to which that participant belongs. The method exposes the participants to structures and regulations utilized for maintaining proper function of a deployed submarine having a plurality of crew members. Each crew member is subjected to a check-in procedure and required to assume ownership of a role. Each crew member must qualify to perform a function associated with the assumed role and each crew member has an assigned ombudsman. The training procedure then equates members of the business organization to which a participant belongs to those crew members. The invention has the advantage of improving performance elements dependent on factors which are of evident importance in a submarine environment but whose central relevance normally remains unnoticed in a normal business organization.

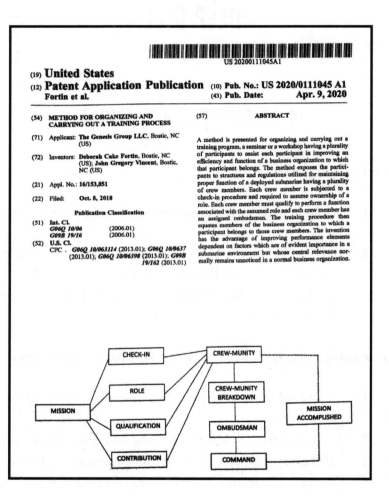

The Patent on the System now published

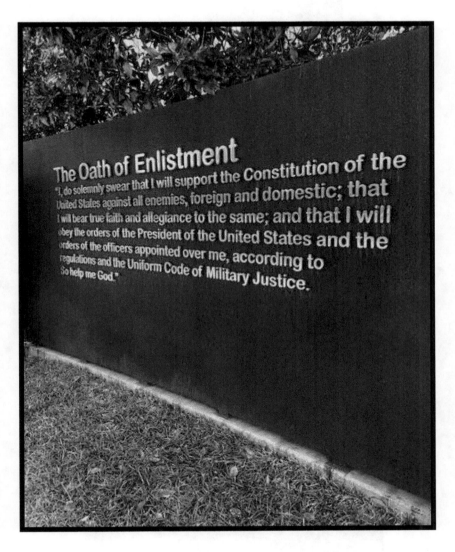

The Oath of Enlistment
"I, do solemnly swear that I will support the Constitution of the United States against all enemies, foreign and domestic; that I will bear true faith and allegiance to the same; and that I will obey the orders of the President of the United States and the orders of the officers appointed over me, according to regulations and the Uniform Code of Military Justice. So help me God."

Oath of enlistment and re-enlistment

Winter in Western NC

Our beloved cabin home Pura Vida

Topside beer break while anchored in the Med

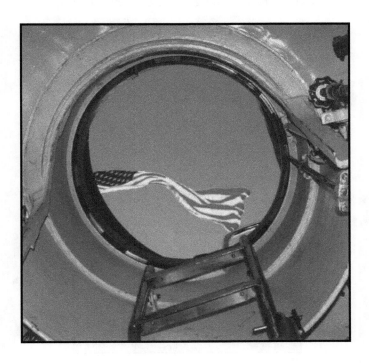

The view from below decks....

Deb capturing thoughts for UP PERISCOPE

9/11 Memorial visit post keynote

The Donald P. Hall fully operational

The Donald P. Hall when I found her....

John's Mom and Dad at his retirement ceremony

Underway, making way, on the Donald P. Hall

View from the Freedom Tower before a Keynote Speech

Torpedos above, bunks below

Deb and Mylee taking a break after an executive session

On our way home after a superb client kick-off in SC

Sometimes John tries to two-step and facilitate

CHAPTER 5

ANCHOR 4: IT IS NOT THE SHIP, SO MUCH AS THE SKILLFUL SAILING THAT ASSURES A PROSPEROUS VOYAGE

Leaders Value What Their People and Others are Good At

So, what are strengths? How does this relatively modern concept fit into over 100 years of submarine service?

| The idea of investing in what people are good at probably started long before it was documented.

Two notable books and theories about this include *Good to Great*, where being in the right seat on the bus is discussed, which means the talent fits the job, inspiring a generation. Gallup took this a lot further, writing several books, beginning with *Soar With Your Strengths* and then *First Break All The Rules*. They developed an assessment that is used to identify and map talents and strengths. Gallup's CliftonStrengths is a valuable scientific assessment but falls short in effectively instructing the user in detail how to use this scientific tool. More on this later in this chapter.

My instincts had long been to place people in roles where they could excel. I followed these instincts for years with great success.

> **My people were happy, engaged, and it showed.**

They were extremely productive and mission-focused. They always got more done than any other team, unit, or group. When I read Jim Collins' *Good to Great* and learned about the right seat on the bus, my mind screamed "Yes!" It was so exciting to have my way of leading validated. When Gallup came out with *Soar with Your Strengths*, they took this a step further and in future books, more steps. I learned with them through my personal experiences and through them by reading. Remember, successful leaders never stop reading and growing.

Today, Deb and I practice strength-based leading with our company, The Submarine Way. Although I was a Gallup fan and had been for years, Deb introduced me to Strengthfinders. She knew her top five talent themes and had been through a strengths executive retreat with her company. Strengthfinders really spoke to me, and a few years later, I worked for Gallup, becoming an expert in Strengthfinders or what is now called CliftonStrengths. We feel strongly that this way of thinking benefits everyone.

In our company, early on, all new associates complete a CliftonStrengths assessment. I like the science behind it and can read an insight report like a technician can read an MRI. I help our new employees understand how they can be the best they can be.

> **My time as a consultant with Gallup honed my natural instincts for placing and developing people in roles where they can take their talents and perfect them into a strength.**

Deb and I take very seriously our need to be consistent with those things we hold to be truths as leaders. Our new associates go through what we called on submarines a qualification card. Nicknamed Qual Card, it is a checklist of everything someone should know about our company. We also created one for our clients and frequently provide it when we are consulting. It assures that all of the first six elements of engagement are covered during check-in/onboarding.

Our organization currently is small and a boutique, which allows us to do a CliftonStrengths on each associate or contractor. No matter how large we become, even when our organization's boutique feel is more culture than reality, we will continue to do assessments and check-in (onboarding), individual mission plans, and seek out the unique talents of every person who works with us. Intentionally developing talents into strengths is powerful beyond words. In many companies we work with today, teaching them to not only put the five pieces of the System in place, of which strengths are one piece, but they must also identify how to value and develop strengths correctly. Excellent leaders look to bring out the best in people, then put structures in place that assure inclusion happens and engagement of the team is sustained. If you have leaders who do not know how to lead through the lens of inclusion, teach them, nurture them, and hire an expert like us. We want to help organizations change their cultures. If you have a leader who is intentionally not inclusive, they must go. They will poison your organization.

I mentioned our proprietary modified 9 Box tool that we use extensively and used in assisting the city in South Carolina with their selection of new leaders and the professional development that would follow. It took a training session and follow-up webinar to get the senior leaders in the mindset of looking beyond current performance to potential. It wasn't an easy transition, but once there, their entire talent pool became available. The person with the most obvious strength for economic development was the first woman to ever be selected for that position; two of the strongest candidates for city manager were African American. This talent-, strength-, and performance-based succession planning were the most out of the box thinking that had ever taken place.

▌ **With unemployment at an all-time low, utilizing and developing existing talent is critical.**

The U.S. Bureau of Labor Statistics projects the need for 1.1 million new nurses by 2024 to replace the 500,000 retiring, and the additional that comes from growth in the industry due to increased need. Do you think keeping the best and ensuring future needs are well resourced will be critical to the healthcare industry in the coming years?

Early in Deb's career, industrial psychologists developed assessments and profiles to help companies identify the right candidates for their jobs. It was recognized that past experience alone was not a good predictor of future success in a job. Over time, companies moved away from this practice for a variety of reasons. Behavioral interviewing replaced these kinds of assessments and profiles, and hiring went on, still a challenge to find the right candidate among hundreds of strangers. Today, thoughtful hiring managers consider talent as a crucial piece of the hiring process. Adding talent-based questions to the behavioral interview process reveals the talents, as well as the experience. Listening closely to responses will also help hiring managers identify when talent is closer to a strength. Experience alone will not create the super team, what we call crew-munity that most organizations desire.

▌ **Crew-munity has tangible benefits to an organization.**

Crew-munity drives return on investment and engagement, which in turn drives return on investment.

We talked earlier about professional development as key to retaining millennials, but that all generations benefit from development and value it. Professional development is one reason average leaders become great leaders, leaders that take their leadership to the next level using strength-based thinking, hiring, and additional professional development. Way beyond culture, latte bars, and rock-climbing walls, good leaders drive engagement in their employees. A company can have an employee-friendly culture, great benefits, fantastic facilities, and still, that one troubled leader can cause a ripple throughout his/her team and among others who intersect with him/her. Strength-based thinking and hiring would likely have this individual on another seat on the bus (or submarine) or not on the bus at all. Sometimes it is necessary.

We talk a lot about inclusion (interdependent collaboration) in this book and the value of leaders who embrace and drive inclusion through the methodology, System, and process, as well as good leadership. So, what role does diversity play in the life of a leader? We've talked about how irrelevant it is that someone is female, gay or African American, Hispanic, or what their religious beliefs are, to what they can accomplish. Focusing on talent and strengths through professional development, starting early in tenure, will assure the building and retention of leaders. Appreciating talent and encouraging collaboration and healthy interdependence drives crew-munity, which means you are much more effective at fighting the submarine.

Strength-based leading improves engagement. What's engagement? Reach for the ceiling instead of just raising your hand when asked. Why is this effort reserved for someone who is engaged? Because being engaged means that most of the time, you are putting that discretionary effort needed to go beyond just being competent to being fantastic. When someone is included, being recognized for their strengths and is operating in a talent area, the results clearly demonstrate the benefit, including an improvement to overall engagement. A Gallup 2016 study listed several of the results: safety incidences were down 70%, turnover decreased by 53%, productivity increased 21%, and sales improved by 20%.

A few words about women on submarines as crew. Women became permanent crew members beginning in 2010, despite space and privacy challenges that included not enough racks and heads for a fully integrated submarine force. The Navy is committed to recruiting the best talent, male or female. In those situations where the submarines have been retrofitted with berthing and heads for women or accommodations for women, it is going well. Retention rates amongst women are very close to those of their male counter-parts. Although there have been a few ugly issues, one well documented in *Diversity and Inclusion The Submarine Way*, the results have been overall very positive. So positive that the next generation of submarines is being designed with key valves and equipment easier to reach for shorter (typically female) crew. Yes, the Navy is designing submarines now with the female crew in mind. I wish they had given this kind of thought to having enough bunks in my day.

Lenny Finds His True North

Lenny E. was an interior communications electrician (IC). What does that mean? It means he showed great promise on his ASVAB, which is the assessment that determines vocation, in that field. Lenny was a very good electrician and a perfectionist. He was frustrated with whoever had designed whatever he worked on, including the electronics on a nuclear submarine. It was like Lenny had electricity running through his brain. Because of this natural talent, layered with perfectionism, he was a nightmare to deal with. Lenny was such a perfectionist that he could not adapt to the lower standards of the electronics on a nuclear submarine. If that sounded tongue in cheek, it was. Lenny was one of those rare individuals who was more talented then what the environment required. Lenny was in the right seat; he was on the wrong bus. Lenny's stay in the Navy was short. He was highly respected for his skill and expertise, but his ability to adapt and collaborate towards a goal was a big problem.

Lenny found his true vocation with me some random day. We were in port and at home in Charleston, visiting a friend's house and drinking beer. Our friend took us out to his new workshop, freshly wired for all the machinery workshops need to run. Lenny took one look at the wiring and exclaimed, "This is not done right." Our friend, with the workshop, asked Lenny how he would do it, and Lenny was off and running. He redesigned the whole thing and the electrician installed it. It was more than perfect. Lenny got out of the Navy, received the appropriate professional designations in electronics, opened his own company, and never looked back.

> Being in the right seat and on the right bus is important to leadership and to general satisfaction in many areas.

Lenny was the kind of leader who had expertise so specific, it had to be done his way, the right way, and he was much happier calling the shots himself. He was in a profession where hiring other pointy people in electronics and hiring a few people who had different skills to run the business aspects of the business worked for him, and he was a happy, grateful leader with a thriving business. Point here, focusing on strengths in leadership is a good first start, but placing people in roles they can excel is a significant piece of this being successful.

Sailor, know thyself

Towards the end of my career in the Navy, although that was, as of that point, unknown to me, I was at Corry Station, running a training command as the Command Master Chief. Although I was suited for a training command, managing the training for over 2000 recruits from different branches of service, it was only my second non-operational responsibility. It took a while for me to realize I was not the tip of the spear and might not ever be again. Being tip of the spear during the Cold War and at the pivotal beginning of my career had certainly left an imprint on me about non-operational roles. After my three years of service there, I began to think about what was next. I dared to dream that I was back on the ocean, maybe an aircraft carrier, but the tip of the spear once again. It was about this time that I was approached by my Force Master Chief, who was overall Naval training. My experience in the Navy on subs meant I had too much sea time, and I would not be assigned to another tip of the spear role. No more sea time for John.

It was determined that I was the prototype of the new senior enlisted in the Navy. I was college-educated, articulate, fit, loved the stage, and was confident. I would go to Washington, and I would be groomed to perhaps become the Master Chief Petty Officer of the Navy down the road. I took the news mostly quietly, knowing this was an honor, a compliment. I was stunned. I would not go back to sea. I listened to the description of the role they had in mind for me, and I could not envision myself in a highly diplomatic/political role in Washington. Over the next few weeks, I thought about what they had in mind for me, and every time I got close to imagining it, I could not quite picture it.

> A guy who values strengths, who believes in leadership both personally and with others, could not embrace a role that was so clearly not a fit.

I decided, after a couple of weeks of consideration, that I could not take the job. I announced I was leaving the Navy I loved, and never looked back. My future held some other career, and my faith in my strengths, and what made me, me, planned my future.

There are a couple of lessons here I wanted to demonstrate through this story. Good leaders understand the difference between an activity not being a preference, or not being a talent area and being a weakness. None of us gets a pass at becoming competent in areas that are weaknesses, but operating in a weak area 80-90% of the day is bound to create an unhappy situation for me and my employer. As much as that new role and the potential path it would put me on was a compliment to me, I was not going to be successful at it. It's also possible that my excellent reputation could be negatively affected. As a leader, it's my responsibility to know myself and the people who report to me, helping them to make good decisions.

In our last book, *Diversity and Inclusion The Submarine Way*, I talked about how the Navy recognized my talent for speaking, and as a result, I was chosen to present to the Under Secretary of the Navy. Although the Navy did not consciously develop strengths, the focus on role vs. just the job allowed a sailor to do more than just the job and expand into areas of talent and strengths. We watched as some sailors struggled in their initial jobs in the Navy. The story of Corey I've discussed many times in speeches and workshops. This young man was close to being thrown out of the Navy. He was hardworking but hadn't found that area of talent needed to get him on track. I recognized what was good about him, went through the steps of the System with him again, (the System is a step-by-step, repeatable system of inclusion that, by the way, has side benefits in meeting goals and achieving missions) check-in, everyone matters if they contribute (strengths) re-introduced him to the crew-mu-nity; I was his ombudsman and got him hyper-focused on the mission. Not all stories end as well as this one, but Corey went on to become successful, became a Navigator, earned his commission, became an officer, and a ship's captain. Going back through the System contributed to his improvement, but focusing on strengths outweighed every other effort.

> If you are struggling with someone's performance, think first about whether they are operating in an area of talent.

In one of Deb's operational roles, seasonal hiring was always challenging. Large numbers of interviews took place, sometimes hundreds at a time. Although there was an effort to hire based on talent, many new associates were brought in by staffing agencies, where there was little screening according to talent. Once in the door, talent became critical to that person's success as it is, quite frankly, in all companies. Each new associate was assigned a program on Day One. They would go through an orientation for the company and the program and meet those individuals critical to the success of their job. After orientation and training, the new associate started their job. About 20% of all new hires were likely not to be successful with the program they were originally assigned. When Deb joined the organization, large numbers of new hires were let go because they were not successful in their new jobs. This was a mismatch of talent to required skills.

Deb began asking questions almost immediately about why a new hire unsuccessful in one program wasn't moved to another program where they could be successful. The program managers, so siloed in their programs, hadn't looked beyond this one individual's lack of success to the bigger picture or asked the question: could someone else have the talent I need? Strength-based thinking looks at all the talent that is available and consciously moves talent to the right job. Deb broke down the silos and got the leaders thinking about all the talent that was available to them.

> Ignite talent while breaking down silos and watch attrition decrease. Employees are happier and customer satisfaction improves. It produces a win/win.

If you focus people on what they love, or at least like a lot, improved engagement results, and a true crew-munity is significantly easier to build.

So how do strengths work? In their introduction to *Now Discover Your Strengths*, Marcus Buckingham and Donald Clifton talk about human beings' fixation with fault and failing and how this does nothing to improve overall performance. Our focus on studying and improving people's faults has done nothing to improve engagement, reduce turnover, or make for a better human being. Most times, it leads to frustration, and it can impact a person's ability to develop a specific strength. Good leaders develop strengths and manage weaknesses and biases while helping those they lead identify talent areas. As we talked about, one way to determine a talent area is through a CliftonStrengths assessment, and for those organizations that want to drive change through their leaders, we highly recommend it. If, for whatever reason, a remote workforce, cost, whatever the reason a CliftonStrengths can't be done, there are other ways to recognize talent areas. Look for how your leader leans into conversations, volunteers for additional responsibility, and runs away from responsibility. This will tell you plenty about what they prefer to do, which is likely a talent area. I jokingly say in workshops, "You don't want me doing financial spreadsheets or detailed Excel spreadsheets. It's fun to watch, but if you want it done fast and right, choose the right talent set."

DEEP DIVE

INTO STRENGTH-BASED LEADERSHIP

Questions to get you thinking:

1. Do you try to know the talents of your people?
2. Do you give them assignments that can help drive talent into a strength?
3. Do your leaders understand the value of strength-based leadership?
4. Do your leaders manage weaknesses?

Three things that help you navigate strength-based leadership:

1. Helping leaders and their people operate in talent areas will improve engagement.
2. There is a return on investment for leaders who help their people operate in areas of talent.
3. Good leaders value strengths and manage biases. If you have a leader who does neither, get rid of him/her. They will poison the organization.

CHAPTER 6

ANCHOR 5: CREW-MUNITY STARTS WITH CREW

L eaders have caring and concern about the people they lead. They want each person to feel valued and be engaged, and for the team to be better than their individual parts. Leaders are not afraid to show they care about each member of the team as an individual. Leaders who are compassionate make the best leaders.

I would say the most significant differentiator of my leadership has been the depth of my caring and my willingness to show it.

If you are a leader who finds it difficult to care about your people, choose another profession. I am not talking about showing that you care. If that's the issue, we can work on it. If you find you focus on your interests exclusively and those of your organization, I will say it again: choose a role where you don't lead people. Selfish leaders are everywhere today. You can tell they are selfish by the chaos around them. They change the strategy based on the way the wind is blowing or to look good. If this sounds like your style, there's time to change but change it now.

It has been several years since I retired from the Navy, but I still hear from those I led. It might be a career change that triggers our conversation, a retirement, or a wedding, but I still hear from my sailors. I also have stayed connected to those I led in the business world. It makes me smile to think about the missions we tackled together, whether it was fighting bad guys in the Atlantic or turning around a failing sales strategy when I got to the CBS television station. I care for them as individuals first, then the contribution they make to the team. Both are critical.

When I am coaching leaders, I am often surprised that sincere caring is difficult for people. Far too often, we are coached to ask how someone is doing today to ask about families or health, which show caring on the surface, and all of that is true; but if caring is not authentic, it will be found out. It is possible to deeply care, be objective, and hold others accountable. Many I coach feel they need to keep their true feelings reserved to preserve objectivity. I would argue that this kind of reserve is detrimental to good leadership. How can you make good decisions about the individual without really understanding them? And how can you focus the individual and the team on a mission without fully understanding their strengths, motivations, and joys? This is revealed through true caring and trust.

Caring Leaders Do Not Take Care of People

| Caring leaders do not take care of their people.

Yes, you heard me right. People who are taken care of do not learn to make independent decisions, or how to handle issues in a crisis and they don't teach others how to develop people to make good decisions or operate independently. Excellent leaders understand they are responsible for an outcome. They understand others are accountable for the outcome as well, but they teach others to get the job done and to get it done right.

Five things a leader can do to teach a person to fish, so they can eat for the rest of their life:

1. Roles and jobs should have talent considerations. Individuals should be placed in jobs where their talents and strengths can contribute.
2. Mistakes happen. We all learn from our mistakes as well as our successes. If individuals do not feel safe to make mistakes, they will not innovate.
3. Give individuals latitude to achieve the mission. If there is no latitude, be honest.
4. Allow individuals access to you to ask questions. Avoid taking over the project. Coach them to a good decision.
5. Make sure there are good plans behind important initiatives, including those that involve developing people.

Authentic caring is demonstrated through genuine relationships with the people the leader interfaces with and leads. These relationships have integrity at the root and are built on an ethical foundation. More to follow on the importance of integrity in leading others. The same with strengths. A good leader knows his/her strengths and looks to maximize these with those they lead. They also look to their people to fill in the gaps created by their lack of expertise in an area.

Truly caring, authentic leaders do not pretend they have expertise in areas they don't.

This isn't caring because it puts everyone at risk. This interdependence also sends a message of inclusion and commitment to the mission and the team. This is likely demonstrated by a passion for the people and the mission. My passion for both was something I couldn't hide, even if I wanted to.

Having a heart as a leader can be a rare attribute. When I asked Deb what her experience was with leaders that had heart, after a 25-year career working for multiple leaders, she could only name two who truly had heart. Both leaders were flawed as people; they were emotional, sometimes held grudges, and were political, but because they cared for their people and their people trusted them to do what was right for them, they were good leaders. Along with caring, consistency of values to action is critical for leaders to demonstrate. Even though these two leaders were flawed, they were perceived as authentic because of these two qualities.

Leaders with heart were also rare in my career, military and otherwise. There was generally some level of compassion there, but sometimes under pressure, it became thinly veiled self-serving leadership. Since I am a positive kind of guy, I have always focused on those leaders who stayed true to themselves and their commitment to us under pressure. Captain Brad McDonald demonstrated caring and consistency under pressure more than any other leader I've ever had.

Captain McDonald Weathers the Storm

Modern submarines are not meant to stay on the surface, especially during severe weather.

Because she is round with no keel, a submarine rocks back and forth, and as wind and waves increase, rolling back and forth becomes more and more problematic to the sailors on the submarine. After hours of being on the surface during this horrible storm in the North Atlantic, all but a few were sick. So sick they took to their bunks and no one could hold any food down. In my fourteen years on boats, it was the worst seasickness episode I've ever witnessed. The few who were left to run the boat were also sick but not bedridden, mostly green around the gills and grumpy as hell. The practical side of the situation was that a few people were maintaining the boat for hours and then throughout the night, with no rest. We asked for permission to submerge and were repeatedly told no. The storm persisted, and the rocking and pitching of the boat continued until those of us with heartier stomachs also were beginning to fail. This was becoming dangerous. The reasons for not submerging are important and—although I can't go into detail; it is still classified—the danger of the boat not being consistently monitored on watch was starting to put us at risk. Keep in mind that watch meant panels and gauges were constantly monitored for anomalies that indicate issues leading to catastrophic failure.

It was one of those situations where leaders need to evaluate the risk of both situations and make a call. Captain McDonald again asked for permission to submerge and was told no. Knowing he was losing his crew, he made a call. We were now in our operating area, but it was too early to submerge. He had the tiny crew left standing check the radar, go active on sonar and our fathometers, basically do whatever we could to let any submarines or ships in the area know we were around and he then gave us the order to submerge the boat.

Captain McDonald cared about the boat, his sailors, and everyone's safety, evaluating the situation that kept us from diving and the consequences of not diving. He made a call that was contrary to his operational orders. Captain McDonald knew he was potentially in trouble, but he cared, and he was the situational leader, who needed to make the call.

> Since I am still here, nothing tragic happened under the ocean that day, and Captain McDonald continued a brilliant tour as our Commanding Officer and years later retired from the Navy, so he was able to explain his decision to his superiors.

Captain McDonald still says you always follow written processes or procedures until you don't. That is leadership, as long as you are right enough, some mistakes are allowed; but in my opinion, he always was right.

There is a difference between compassion and sympathy. Compassion is a feeling of empathy for another's suffering and the desire to relieve that suffering. Sympathy is a feeling of pity and sorrow for someone else's misfortune. Don't get caught up in sympathy and pity without considering what it might take to alleviate that suffering. Remember the Chinese proverb: "You give a poor man a fish, and you feed him for a day. When you teach him to fish, you give him an occupation for a lifetime." So, what does this say about the compassionate leader? It says that accountability, coaching, and teaching are also necessary, as well as listening to issues or problems. Earlier, we talked about the tough, young man, Corey. With support, he became fully accountable for the results that were expected from him and for his future. With compassionate leadership, he had a very successful future with the Navy.

> In our course on compassionate leadership, we teach students of leadership to appreciate the value of silence.

Often this silence is about learning how to listen. If you are a high energy leader who is all about getting things done, really listening might have to be intentional for you. I always suggest, and we teach in our course for leaders, to first just be silent when someone is talking, sharing, and opening up. Meeting someone's eye and allowing them to open up without comment deepens trust. We have an exercise during this course where individuals in a breakout session practice talking about emotional, personal stories, while everyone remains silent, not commenting. This exercise teaches leaders to be intentional leaders who listen first to show compassion. We also talk about what the fouled anchor means to compassionate leadership. More on listening later, but it is critical to compassion.

The fouled anchor, U.S.N. its definition and then the interpretation of what all of it means I teach through the lens of a compassionate leader.

The U in USN stands for unity, cooperation, harmony, and continuity of purpose and action. The S stands for service to God, fellow man, and the Navy. The N stands for navigation, which reminds us to keep ourselves on a true course before all mankind.

The chain is symbolic of flexibility and reminds us of the chain of life we forge with honor, morality, and virtue. It is wrapped, or "fouled," acknowledging that there will be challenges on our path; things will not always go as we plan or desire them to go.

In one of our most popular programs, I ask, "What kind of responsibility does this mean you have as a leader? How does a leader unify? Is equity an important value? How about listening? Does a good leader listen to unify, and to create harmony? What is the root emotion necessary to lead with honor, morality, and virtue?" Well, it is more than just the qualities mentioned here, but leading with compassion is an important component of leading effectively and, in our opinion, is the root of honor, morality, and virtue. Like the Fouled Anchor shows, we should lead through the trials and tribulations we face; understanding all humans have trials and tribulations is the key to compassion.

The quote below came from *Diversity and Inclusion The Submarine Way*, where we discuss in detail that leadership is a critical anchor to all things inclusive. "Promoting a leader who is all head and no heart will always be a struggle. You might get temporary results, but the big picture will be compromised." What does this quote mean? It means you cannot walk away from accountability, which is the head, the result; but without heart when dealing with people, you eventually will become ineffective. What is the eventual result of having no heart in your leadership style? Loyalty will be compromised. You will not get the commitment you need to complete the mission. Period.

Integrity in Leadership

I mentioned integrity earlier, and as part of the fouled anchor, integrity is described as honor, morality, and virtue. Integrity is still described as one of the most important leadership qualities. Integrity in leadership is usually described as a deep commitment to doing the right thing for the right reason. It also means even if the situation is unpleasant, the truth must be spoken. In this context, we are talking about leaders and their employees. The other important factor is leaders who demonstrate integrity in business relationships to partners, vendors, mergers, and transactions. Without integrity, employee and business relationships will be compromised. When leaders have integrity, employees and business associates associate integrity with kindness and good intentions rather than selfish intentions. As a result, the business is a lot more likely to grow and weather hard times.

Five Ways to Demonstrate Integrity

1. Compassion/kindness shows integrity and respect for people.

2.   Leaders are accountable as well as holding others accountable. They walk the talk.

3.   Being honest and even vulnerable shows integrity.

4.   Making decisions that keep equity in mind. Fair used to mean equal; today it means equity. What one person needs, another might not.

5.   Practice non-judgment and don't lead with bias. Appreciating people for their talent, strengths, and contribution first manages bias.

How a Leader Communicates

> In my view, it is not possible to be a great leader without also having mastery over communication.

It does not have to be polished with a large vocabulary, but it does need to be clear and, if needed, actionable. In the next section, I talk more about listening, as the communication of an effective leader does involve as much listening as talking. Another trait a successful leader has in their communication style is to speak with passion. This usually involves painting a vivid picture of the situation they are bringing attention to, which includes evoking emotion in their listener. In our first book, *Diversity and Inclusion The Submarine Way*, I talk about the difficult conversation I had with Corey, the young man separating from the Navy and how I used vivid, emotion-evoking language to get his attention and shake him up. The rest is a very positive story for him and the Navy, but without this communication, Corey would have separated from the Navy and led a very different life.

Five Critical Communication Traits

1.   Talk and listen with openness and manage bias.
2.   Ask for feedback on what you've communicated. Restate if communication isn't clear.
3.   When talking to a group, set a time limit and an agenda and stick by it. You will not lose listeners unless you have a reputation for rambling.
4.   Just like the anchors of leadership, communicate to the individual first and the group next. People hear and respond as individuals.
5.   Talk in vivid language, show excitement and passion. Ignite the conversation with your enthusiasm.

The Importance of Verbatim Repeat Back to Communication

What we can learn from precision communication?

Imagine this exchange between the Officer of the Deck (OOD), the Diving Officer (DO), the inboard station (FW) and the outboard station (SP) while changing depth:

OOD: Diving officer, make your depth 400 feet.
DO: Make my depth 400 feet, aye.
DO: Full rise on the fairwater planes.
FW: Full rise on the fairwater planes, aye.
DO: 10 degree up bubble.
SP: 10 degree up bubble, aye.
DO: Officer of the deck, 700 feet, coming to 400 feet.
OOD: Very well, dive.
DO: Officer of the deck, passing to 600 feet, coming to 400 feet.

OOD: Very well, dive.

DO: Officer of the deck, passing to 500 feet, coming to 400 feet.

OOD: Very well, dive

DO: Full dive on the fairwater planes.

FW: Full dive on the fairwater planes, aye.

DO: Zero bubble.

SP: zero bubble, aye.

DO: Take control of your fairwater planes; make your depth 400 feet.

FW: Take control of my fairwater planes and make my depth 400 feet, aye.

FW: Dive, at 400 feet.

DO: Officer of the deck, at 400 feet.

OOD: At 400 feet, aye dive.

Verbatim communication here doesn't exist in the business world. Is there any room for interpretation here, even if you don't exactly know what some of this terminology means? What if business goals or performance feedback was this crisp? Unfortunately, often clarification for specific direction comes in the form of "Do you understand . . . ," with most people telling you they do, because they are uncomfortable telling you they don't. How would someone understand this direction:

"Brenda, it is important that we provide incremental onboarding training to that new team that started last week. As you know, onboarding is critical. Tell me exactly who, why, and where you will be conducting the training when we meet tomorrow morning. Now, Brenda, tell me what I expect tomorrow morning when we meet."

In this scenario, Brenda plays back what I've told her I expect, giving us a chance to determine if she really does understand all the details.

> You will not sound like, nor should you be a verbatim repeat-back manager, but it is not enough to ask someone if they understand. You must be specific about what they understand to surface clarity issues.

The Compassionate Listener

We talked earlier about the value of listening to further relationships and build trust. The opposite is someone who talks all the time, interrupts, and takes over conversations.

> When we finally decide as a leader that a person is hopelessly rude, and we see it on everyone's face, it must be handled carefully.

Not handling the situation starts a blame game and accusations from all the team begin to fly. Before this happens, pause, stay empathetic and ask the person if you can speak freely. Let them know you'd like to contribute to the conversation and others would like to as well. Explain that a two-way conversation is the most effective way to communicate, and you would like to participate in an on-the-level discussion with them. If you find these kinds of traits slip into your communication style, you need to be very intentional when you talk and listen, so you manage this tendency.

One-sided conversations did happen on a submarine, and they were not always pleasant and usually involved colorful language. There were plenty of rude people who never listened and wanted to monopolize conversations. Our conversations were more direct than compassionate, but remember my statement earlier: "I don't have to like you, but I do have to love you." Creating a culture of listening, clear communication, and openness was far too important for us not to address this issue.

> Managing those who do not value compassionate listening allows those leaders who have mastered the skill and understand the value to set the tone for the culture.

So, let's get this out there. I was a tough leader who expected a lot from his people. I still do. As tough as I was, I felt it important to stop and listen with compassion when compassion was required. One important thing to make a note of regarding compassionate listening is to initially listen without judgment. This means to quickly determine the reason for the conversation, and if you feel the purpose is to gain empathy first, the path to the conversation is different than I am stating here. Second, don't immediately try to fix the problem. Many of us are problem solvers by nature. Avoid this initially. Third, don't get defensive if the issue is related to your responsibility. Be open, and mostly quiet, except for asking clarifying questions. If you have determined this is an issue that can be fixed and the solution is agreed to, take the necessary steps. Otherwise, compassionate listening is just that, listening.

Deck Plate Leaders

You could ask, "What the heck is a deck plate leader?" and I wouldn't think the question odd. It is a very strange term for someone never on a sub. The term servant leader is overused and unclear, but my version of that is the deck plate leader. Let's start with a deck plate. Simply put, it's the deck on a sub. Conversations in the goat locker (chief's quarters) were always about what the rank and file thought, or those on the deck plate. Getting inside their head, understanding and listening to the concerns and the observations of the sailors was a daily conversation in the goat locker. So, the common definition of a servant leader is to serve, share power, and put the need of the employee first. Let me tackle that from the goat locker.

Servant Leaders Viewed from the Goat Locker

There are many who see the servant leader not as serving others but teaching others to help themselves. The goat locker (where the chief petty officers live) conversations are not only all about the crew, but all about the crew learning to be self-sufficient. This was very ingrained in me not just through instincts but also through training. Next, sharing power: power should not be the focus since whoever is the expert should be the person to lead the discussion in a credible way and drive the project. A symphony of leadership means the perfect ebb and flow, mostly of the experts. This is based on the experts weighing in on topics we've covered in other chapters. When it comes to a final call on an issue, there is one person in power, and that means one throat to choke. You own your decision; sometimes alone and sometimes as a department or division of decisionmakers, but it is yours and yours alone when the situation requires it. I've read articles from the goat locker online, and there is a thread through the community, different than when I served, of the chiefs who have given up power.

> Chiefs, by and large, were selected because they had a directness, documented success and expertise in both technical applications as well as personnel development that contributed to the overall mission.

They spoke their minds to both those who reported to them and those they reported to. You could always get an honest, straight answer from a chief. There are a variety of reasons, but some chiefs feel they are being forced into political roles, where being agreeable is more important than the truth as a chief sees it. It worked when a chief knew integrity and commitment to the creed was the clearest definition of leadership. It seems that leadership all over has become diluted with politics.

| My clear request is for a leader to do what's right, even when it is difficult to do.

Compassionate Leadership is About Going the Extra Mile

Physical training was required in the Navy, called PT; not just with the Navy, but with every branch of the military. Come to think of it; we called it that in high school, too. It consisted of a certain number of sit-ups, push-ups, and running a mile in a specific amount of time. It also consisted of at least some monitoring of weight to height ratios. So, my compassion was challenged with another chief—although I was Chief of the Boat—who had failed both PT and his height/weight ratios. Now, keep in mind that, on a fast attack, PT was very difficult. On some boats, there was a rowing machine, and many sailors did dips, push-ups, and pull-ups in the torpedo room or wherever they could find the room; but in general, there was no space for keeping fit aerobically. I was super committed to it, so I found every opportunity to work out in whatever conditions, but again, it was not easy.

This chief had failed the height/weight ratio and was really overweight. Ironically, although he was a very good performer, if he didn't lose weight, he was going to be separated after sixteen years of service. He had tried everything to lose weight. On a submarine, food was available all the time because of all the shifts being served, so imagine having fresh cookies, pizza at midnight, and breakfast starting at 0600 with full meals every six hours, available 24/7. To make it even tougher, the food was very good. You could literally eat whenever you weren't sleeping, and few slept very much. So, I naturally assumed this chief had succumbed to the temptations of food. I reached out to him, offered my help, and he accepted it. This was not a leadership role that was in any way glamorous. My first suggestion was to ask him to log his food and drink intake. I told him not to focus on losing weight but just logging his food.

I was known for being super fit and making that a priority, ironic when I considered I both smoked two packs of cigarettes a day for years and drank a great deal but approached healthy food and exercise with passion. After one week of this chief's food and drink being logged, I was surprised by the volume of fruit and vegetables and lean meats. It was particularly perplexing. Why was he overweight? Then I noticed the amount of sugary beverages he was drinking. He was drinking over a liter a day. My next step was to ask him to eliminate and replace his soda with unsweetened tea or coffee. Water was also acceptable. In one month, he lost fifteen pounds. This was not glamorous leadership, and it never got a lot of attention, but caring takes all kinds of forms, and this salvaged this chief's career.

| The biggest impact on leadership might not have any glamor.

This chief took it from there, stayed on his water and tea diet, and became quite fit. I helped, which is all some people need, and he did the rest.

DEEP DIVE

INTO COMPASSIONATE LEADERSHIP

Questions to test your knowledge:

1. What are the five critical communication traits?
2. What are the five ways to demonstrate integrity?
3. What are the five things a leader can do to teach a person to fish?

Three things to navigate achieving the mission:

1. Listening builds trust and improves relationships.
2. Effective leaders care and show it.
3. One-sided rude communication needs to be addressed.

CHAPTER 7

WHEN THE SAILS FIND PERFECT WINDS

When Leadership Comes Together in a Perfect Symphony

Accountability, collaboration, interdependence, and overall leadership often must come together in a perfect symphony. We have talked about how a submarine crew of 110 on a fast attack completely turns over every three years and yet the mission is not impacted, nor is the operation of the boat itself. How difficult would this be to duplicate in the private sector? From our experience, this would be nearly impossible as the private sector operates today. In this environment, there is an even higher level of interdependence and collaboration (our definition of inclusion) and the leadership required.

Considering a three-year turnover model is challenging, missile submarines (those capable of carrying ballistic missiles) have two separate crews (usually one is called Blue and the other Gold) to operate the submarine. Literally, 150 people share the submarine to keep it at sea for longer periods of time. This would be like one company having two totally separate staffs, and every three to four months, one staff comes in and replaces the other staff in total. The business keeps operating smoothly and the customers see no effect on the product or service. Perhaps they just notice different faces.

So how long do you think it takes to completely turn over a nuclear submarine capable of carrying ballistic missiles? Thousands of pieces of paper and records to review, stacks of maintenance requirements, and literally every single aspect of effectively operating a nuclear submarine are turned over to entirely new staff. How long do you think the turnover takes? Not long. During the period of turnover, the previous crew and the new crew are working together to do the repairs on the boat, update the new crew on the mission, and get it ready to head out. Within two weeks, there's a 100% turnover of the boat to the new crew. Thirty days later, the new crew is back out to sea, operating a nuclear submarine. The amount of intense leadership, communication, and collaboration involved is off the charts. Although every crew leaving says they disclose even the smallest issue, every crew coming on says many items were hidden or overlooked. "Sandbagging" is legendary in the world of missile boats. Regardless of this, the submarine is back in the water, fulfilling the mission.

> Complaining was normal, and we even had an expression for it: "A bitching sailor is a happy sailor."

Cascading Leadership

These turnovers are perhaps the best example of cascading leadership and the symphony of leadership mentioned earlier. The two commanding officers need to go over a massive amount of information, and the most junior supervisor is doing the exact same thing with their counterparts, and so all the roles go. The power here is that *every* level must work effectively. We are, after all, talking about a nuclear submarine capable of carrying nuclear ballistic missiles. The risks are high if everyone isn't doing their job, their role, and leading effectively. So how specifically is it done? First and foremost, we have and rely on extremely detailed processes and procedures to leave nothing to memory or chance. There are checklists and daily briefings on what is on track and what is behind, and sometimes more-than-daily briefings. Secondly, the expertise of the leaders is critical, as well as leadership itself. Knowing what to ask, what to look for, what is really a big issue, and what is a minor one.

> High-reliability organizations succeed based on trusting the lowest accountable level expert to run things and handle the big issues. More on high-reliability organizations later, but Naval Aviation says they first developed high reliability and the Submarine Force says we did; of course, we did, but regardless, we both use it and it works.

Those issues are run by leadership at the appropriate level to make sure there are no surprises and that the right people weigh in. Then they own the issue and drive it to resolution.

When it comes to being prepared to be one of these leaders at whatever level, nothing is left to chance. You learn every piece of equipment or every nuance of your role and workspace starting the first days you ever set foot on a boat. You watch others more senior and hear the questions they ask. You observe the way they inspect equipment and review paperwork. You also observe leadership styles and work on the one that fits you. You follow their lead, work hard, study, and soon, you too are an expert. What is amazing is mid-level or senior-level leaders that have never been on a missile boat; only fast attacks (fast attacks have just one crew) still go through this process effectively, although they have never done it before. How is this possible? Back to leading through the lens of inclusion. We all are dependent on others who may be junior in rank but senior in expertise. We also count on the collaboration and assistance of our counterparts to perhaps take a bit more time to explain things and point out areas that are critical to the operation of the boat underway. It is the best example of the symphony of leadership I have ever seen, anywhere in or out of the Navy. "We don't have to like each other," I always say in my keynotes, "but we do have to love each other." When you know that someone truly has your back, it's a game-changer.

What if every business, every community, made a commitment that their leaders would work together for the betterment of the community or business despite the differences? When leaders finally make a commitment not to let partisanship get in the way of making the best decisions, then leaders can begin to work together in this symphony of leadership that contributes to exceeding the individual or isolated decisions coming out of leaders.

Our friends in healthcare understand the value of high reliability. Many health organizations teach it, expect it, and hold their teams accountable for it. A hospital system we work with in Atlanta truly exemplifies high reliability for safety. Their nurses or assistants are not afraid to speak up if it means their patients could be at risk. The best example of this is a nurse who notices a doctor prescribing a medicine a patient would be allergic to. Instead of keeping quiet, the nurse points it out, averting a serious situation. High reliability requires all levels to lead. It requires all to lead. Having leaders only at the top puts the organization at risk.

So, exactly what is high reliability, and why is every level ready to lead in an HRO (high-reliability organization)? HROs— first introduced, then perfected in the Navy—are organizations that operate in complex, error-prone, fast-changing, extreme stress environments, where the consequences are high if there is a problem. Regardless, these organizations operate without serious accidents or failures. A nuclear accident on a submarine would be a perfect example of where the consequences would be high if there was an accident. Operating a nuclear reactor under the ocean and, in fact, operating a submarine, the most sophisticated, complex, and dangerous vessel in the world, nuclear accident-free for 60-plus years is noteworthy. Add the fact that the average age on board is 23, 90% of the crew is under 35, and 80% only have high school educations, and I would recommend every organization in the world study how success and safety are achieved on submarines. Need more? Remember, nearly 100% of the crew changes over every three years. Noteworthy now approaches unbelievable, but it is absolutely true. High reliability is the norm on a submarine. Each individual lead is responsible for safety, and each has an obligation to point out failure. Organizations are much more effective if they build and expect leadership from all levels.

> Many of our clients are frustrated that their mid-level managers don't lead, make as few decisions as possible, and are focused on the job, not the role.

What does focus on role vs. job mean? On submarines, if there is a fire on board, we don't wait around for the fire department to come and put out the fire; whoever is there and trained on firefighting (which is everyone) puts out the fire. To wait around for whoever is officially responsible for putting out the fire puts the submarine at risk. All jobs are viewed from the lens of roles vs. jobs. A submarine sailor never—yes, never—has just one role on a submarine. Even if a sailor is still being trained on watch, they don't only just train. They wash dishes, clean toilets, and fill in wherever they are needed. In business, a mid-level manager who leads a team could also coordinate onboarding, be a mentor to someone, or write technical specs.

The more mid-level managers go beyond the job to the role, the more likely they are to operate in an area of talent or strength. They are also more likely to feel like they have autonomy in an area where they can really lead. Allow mid-level managers to choose their role and watch them become more comfortable with leading. Then make sure mid-level managers are developed to be good leaders. Remember, we said that good leaders are not only innate leaders, but it's critical they are developed to be excellent leaders. To avoid development could lead to talented, natural leaders making potentially serious mistakes they are not able to recover from.

So, why do so many organizations feel their mid-level managers could step up more, role model, hold others accountable, and drive resolution of issues?

There are specific things we coach our clients to consider regarding their mid-level managers:

1. Provide broad direction and allow leaders to grow into a role that suits them.
2. Don't focus on personal failure while neglecting a focus on positive qualities and results.
3. Focus leaders on the mission of the organization. Make sure they understand their part in the mission, role, not just job.
4. Provide professional development to your developing managers and refresher training to your experienced managers.

> Many organizations unintendedly build leaders who are good at carrying out the orders of their superiors but do not contribute much in adapting, pushing back when the decision could be harmful or explaining these decisions to the people who must carry them out.

Decisions that could be harmful to the organization are often made because the person that is making them is not close to the heartbeat of the people who work there. Anyone leading a large organization can get further and further away from the tactical executers if allowed to. They must seek input, and the people who work for them must provide that input. If there is a circle of leadership, hypothesis>input from key individuals>modify decision and communication>input from other key decisionmakers>execute> then decisions get modified or even eliminated before they can do harm.

Circle Of Leadership

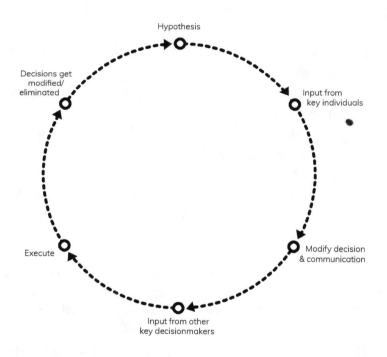

Hypothesis

Decisions get
modified/
eliminated

Input from
key individuals

Execute

Modify decision
& communication

Input from other
key decisionmakers

Running Aground Submerged

When I speak or write about the lowest level of accountability and the importance of it, this situation is the first that comes to mind. We were in restricted waters, with a lot of seamounts, so it was a very dangerous situation. We were submerged and could not go up to periscope depth because of where we were. To make matters more stressful, we had a catastrophic failure of our inertial navigation system, which tells us what our course and estimated position is underwater. The only thing we had to operate with was a mark 19 gyro, which was accurate. It would provide the known direction we were going, but the golden rule of navigation is you don't use just one heading source for navigation. We had another source: a mark 27 gyro, the same heading gyro on an Abrams tank.

| We called it an R2D2 (Star Wars reference), and it was in the laundry area.

We frankly didn't pay much attention to it because it was always plus or minus 3-4 degrees, so not very accurate.

The Auxiliary Electrician Watch, as part of their rounds every hour would call up to the Quartermaster stand and check all gyros. The Quartermaster was navigating the boat, and if there was ever a time someone could convince themselves things were too hectic to check the gyro, this would have been it. I chose to have all heading sources on the ship's control panel selected to the MK 19. I consciously chose not to show the MK 27 (R2D2), which would have been prudent and required. I did this because R2D2 was not very accurate, but that limited me to one heading source. Our heading from the one gyro showed due north, and we were going very fast. The compass heading was 000. There are several issues going on, and given the situation, we had the latitude to skip certain procedures if a note was made of it. R2D2, the mark 27 gyro, was a prime candidate for not following through on because of the other issues. The twenty-year-old, high school-educated Auxiliary Electrician (AE) did not agree. It needs to be understood that the Auxiliary Electrician (AE) is a lower-ranking individual with little "authority." When the AE called the Quartermaster and insisted on providing the R2D2 reading, the Quartermaster commented, "Dude, do you know what I am dealing with here?"

When the AE finally convinced the Quartermaster to take the reading, we discovered that the primary mark 19 gyro said we were going 001, while the tank gyro, affectionately known as R2D2, said we were going 270, due west. They are never that far off from each other. The Quartermaster coordinated with the officer of the deck, and we stopped the submarine in the middle of the ocean. The mark 19 had locked itself in place, appearing to go due north, which is a default setting. Reality is that we were going due west and heading toward a rock cliff at 20 knots submerged.

> We would have faced a catastrophic collision had that young AE had not insisted we check the obsolete gyro, and because of his insistence and his leadership, we averted a disaster. The point of the story: everyone can lead, and it's critical everyone has an opportunity to state their case. It's not a title or money; it's about contribution and value.

Focus on the Mission

Good leaders are always aware of the mission. Good leaders define the mission for others, constantly clarifying and communicating changes. Defining the mission could be a quarterly exercise or a daily reminder of what the purpose of the team is. Frequently is better, but ultimately the communication is related to the length and the complexity of the mission. In *Diversity and Inclusion The Submarine Way*, we talk about the Four Steps for Achieving the Mission:

Acceptance: Acknowledge and welcome new people into the mission. New people bring new ideas and differences into the environment, which can open new ways to accomplish the mission. When boots hit the steel deck for the first time, the expectation is that they contributed to the mission, immediately.

Embrace what you can't change because your mission is an order: Decide what is important to you and state your case. If the case does not have merit according to the command, move on. If anything interferes with the mission, it's your duty to speak up.

Steady State: Once you've stated your case, the mission stays the same or is modified, and planning for the mission is in place, you reach a steady state. A steady-state that ignores new input or changing criteria, however, risks the mission. Steady-state must stay ready to change in light of new circumstances.

Readiness, the state of being fully prepared for something: A culture of readiness is not an easy one to build or sustain. Steady state is a status that remains unchanged unless a willingness to be open to changing input happens. Readiness is preparation for significant change that could impact the outcome of the mission.

We often train with police and police leaders. Steady state, readiness, and focus on the mission are all areas we cover repeatedly. Police who are not prepared for the unusual or view situations based on personal biases put themselves and others in jeopardy. Readiness keeps police on alert for changes to circumstances that require them to adapt.

Four Critical Steps to Readiness

Identify the result of the readiness state in advance. How would success be defined?

For example, if the desired readiness is to have a plan should there be a blackout, so police immediately know how to handle looting, robbery or violent crime and know to deploy this approach immediately should a blackout happen, start with the end in mind, as Covey would say. Is success, police hit the streets, certain areas, blocks using non-violent tools, reducing potential crime through their efforts? You could even get more specific, adding percentages and outcomes. Once the end has been defined, build the readiness plan.

Identify the accountable person for the result.

Once the owner of a result is correctly identified, it is easier to cascade the mission and the plan for readiness to the organization. This demonstrates the importance of accountability but also demonstrates appropriate leadership.

Identify team members to communicate the readiness plan, the training, and the outcome.

The individuals who communicate the plans need to be completely bought into the plan, good communicators, and vested in the outcome of the readiness plan.

The new culture must be described, and the new behaviors integrated into daily activities to drive change.

Drilling (training) the required changes frequently assures that there's preparation for the readiness plan. Just like a tornado drill and a fire drill prepare people for what to do in an emergency, drilling for readiness does the same thing. Exceptional leadership is not just focusing on the mission, but readiness when the mission goes awry.

In leadership circles, choosing a high-performing leader is critical.

If you choose a high-performing leader, the average of the team goes up.

So, when you want to improve the team, choose the right leader. Recruiters search endlessly when the job is tough for the right leader. They conduct countless interviews and check backgrounds for the spark they expect to see in a leader candidate. There are several ways to identify someone who is the right leader and who will raise the average of the team. Does this individual focus on the potential, the opportunities? Is that where they spend their time? What excites them about your opportunity, regardless of how challenging it is? Do they lean in to hear more? Do they see people as potential, getting excited to move them to the right spot to achieve more? And if that potential leader is you, how are you responding?

Situational Leadership Should be Tied to Readiness

There are many articles and books about situational leadership. Some of them are fantastic and some not so much. My comment on situational leadership's importance is this: situational leadership allows the leader and those who are part of the leader's team to apply leadership characteristics to the group primarily based on their readiness. That is why we went into so much detail on readiness in the previous part of this chapter. This readiness is based on the readiness of the individual and of the team. The leader then decides what and how to give more responsibility to the individual and team based on this readiness.

The situational leader 1) is mission-focused but puts emphasis on the role of the individual in the mission; 2) targets employee development to the individual and the needs of the mission; 3) teaches leaders to assess the situation and adjust accordingly; and 4) communicates in a way that influences the results and helps to achieve the mission.

The situational leader is also able to tap into all leaders, superiors, peers, and individual leaders in a way that influences the outcome.

> They take advantage of and benefit from other leaders to create a beautiful symphony of leaders.

DEEP DIVE

INTO PERFECT SYMPHONIES OF LEADERSHIP

Questions to test your knowledge:

1. What are the four critical steps to readiness?
2. What are the four steps of achieving the mission?
3. What is the lesson in running aground submerged?
4. What are the four things leaders should know about their mid-level managers?

Three things to navigate achieving the mission:

1. Readiness planning is critical to achieving the mission.
2. High reliability assures there's leadership at all levels.
3. The mission must be tied to the role, not just a job for truly effective leadership.

CHAPTER 8

WHEN LEADING IS DIFFICULT

"Those that will not sail until all dangers are over will never put to sea." – Dr. Thomas Fuller

ecause of a variety of reasons, leading can be difficult. In our bestselling first book, *Diversity and Inclusion The Submarine Way*, we discuss the issue of several women officers being videotaped in the shower on the USS *Wyoming* by enlisted sailors. This videotape spread off *Wyoming* to other boats and was viewed by several other sailors on and off *Wyoming*. When we talked about the issues in *Wyoming*, we spent most of our time talking about the impact of a breakdown in norms. This was a black eye on the Navy, and a breakdown in norms is a critical issue, but not the only issue.

Leading in these circumstances is difficult. Keep in mind I said difficult, not impossible.

It is hard to know all the details in this environment, but a new and, even more than new, a significant change had been introduced to the USS *Wyoming* and to the submarine force. Women, except for special circumstances, were not on submarines until 2010, when the first female supply officer joined the USS *Ohio*. The USS *Wyoming* incident occurred in 2014, so not that long after the overall decision to allow female officers on board. So why bring this up again? Because leading is often not easy. Just a few of the changes on board included space, like sleeping quarters, the head; privacy, (a few sailors slept naked during my fifteen years on subs, so I'm sure that was a consideration) and on and on. There are several white papers and courses out there about leading difficult people; for example, people you wouldn't or didn't hire, but what do you do when the circumstances make leading difficult, leading to difficult situations?

In the last couple of decades, Navy SEALs have received a good deal of publicity. The Navy SEALs in the news today, the one the Navy retired after posing with an ISIS teenager he had killed, in violation of the Uniform Code of Military Justice article 134, I see as a symptom of an internal issue. There are bad apples in every field, but the consequences of a bad apple in the Navy SEALs are staggering.

Put a high-powered rifle in the hands of someone with issues, and you have a volatile situation.

I worked with SEALs for three years while stationed on the Navy's first Dry Deck Shelter submarine. I came to know and respect their allegiance to each other, and their respect for strength-based teamwork. They called each other by their first names with little outward recognition of rank.

Something similar happened during my time on subs when VIP cruises carrying important people from the private sector would get underway with us. It always made me feel a bit uncomfortable. It was hard to focus on fighting the submarine when you were performing a dog and pony show. My summary is this: if, as a leader, your motivation is anything other than the goal of the mission, danger is nearby. Publicity of any special operations unit or mission can have negative consequences and sometimes attract players that shouldn't be a part of the team. Although VIP cruises were a pain, I never would have met Wayne Huizenga, Jr. if it hadn't been for one of them. We had a lot of fun in those years. To all of us, he was a regular guy who needed to take his turn buying the beer, and he did. His life has changed, and so has mine, but those years forged my view of leadership.

When I was a Command Master Chief, at the training command, I had a Commanding Officer initially who only wanted to better the training and keep the joint command engaged. We did some incredible work together. We took a training command that had received some of the worst feedback in the Navy to one that received the best feedback within a year and a half.

When this CO was relieved by someone who was more focused on the command as a showplace, our success leveled off. Leadership should never be about the recognition of the leader, but about continuous focus on the mission.

Recognition of good leaders happens, but that should not be the motivation of the leader.

Two Sailors

"There are only two Sailors, in my experience, that never ran aground: one never left port, and the other was an atrocious liar" (Don Bonford). I love this quote because it speaks my truth. Running aground in leadership happens to all of us. In the situation of *Wyoming*, she ran aground with all on board. It was a serious breach of ethics and leadership. How could this difficult change for the submarine force have been handled better? It was difficult for everyone, including the female officers, other officers, the captain and the enlisted sailors. We offer the Navy this idea: have a chief sponsor the new female officer(s) immediately upon coming on board. Chiefs have street cred, and the minute some-one gets out of line, that chief, tapped into the crew, can address it. The breakdown onboard the USS *Wyoming*, if we learn from it, should never happen again. The female officers don't need protec-tion; they are tough enough. They need an introduction, a sponsor, and support from those who have street cred. All that being said, retention of female officers is similar to that of male officers on a submarine, 26% of females retained and 27% for males.

In 2010, the Navy wrote an article about the health hazards of women on a nuclear submarine, including the effect on any fetus should the woman get pregnant before or during deployment. The concerns were dark, almost prohibitive. Real or not real, I don't know, but focusing on the downside and not on the upside of a diverse crew serves no purpose except for dealing with the reality of the challenges.

> In 2019, women are successfully serving onboard submarines and the comment, "they just want to be submariners," not women submariners rings true with me. When you focus on talent, leadership and contribution, driving inclusion, difficult leadership, and difficult circumstances get perspective.

Winston Churchill famously said, "When you are going through hell, keep going." Lesson learned here is that if you are in the crosshairs as a leader or the team is in the crosshairs, con-tinue to execute your plan. Stopping to test a new concept doesn't make sense at this stage. That doesn't mean you don't make tacti-cal changes along the way. It means that a huge change in strategy happens when you've crossed your way out of hell, not into the opposite necessarily but at least into a moment of calm when you can regroup. At this point, reevaluate your strategy and determine if it is working. We can all come up with ways things can't work, but a high functioning leader determines what does work, or why it isn't working, so they can adjust the sails.

My Experience at Leading When it was Hard

Fraternity initiations (hazing) have gotten a lot of attention over the last few years, with incidents ranging from benign pranks to some tragic consequences like alcohol poisoning and behavior rising to the level of abuse.

> The chief's initiation was also a potential problem, which is why when I had the authority to, I decided to modify or stop it.

The chief's initiation was very popular, and what I wanted to do not so much. But let's first talk about what the chief's initiation was. It was supposed to be a structured three-month transition from petty officer to chief, which as you've read comes with a significant change of expectations. The chief's initiation, however, had degraded into an alcohol-fueled, unbridled three months of craziness, intertwined with some real-life transitioning. In my opinion, there was too little of that and way too much of the alcohol-fueled shenanigans. I participated in it as a chief-to-be, because I'm a fun guy and there was enormous pressure to participate. Maybe I even brought a few laughs to it, but all the while, I had committed myself to change it when I had the authority.

I made big changes six years later when I became Chief of the Boat (think the senior-most enlisted on board) on the USS *Pennsylvania*. I finally had enough authority that I could now restructure this event that I had come to dislike quite a bit, so the transition to chief had meaning during every day of the transition, not just on the day anchors were pinned on you. The first thing I did was to eliminate alcohol during the initiation activities. This was extremely unpopular. The second thing I did was to structure coaching sessions for the selectees, so they had an opportunity to learn about being a chief. Probably the most unpopular thing I did, because the impact was on a wide variety of individuals, was to eliminate my chief selectees' participation in the alcohol-infused initiation activities during joint initiations. Many initiations were shared with other subs, so the activities could be scaled. One sub might have one, two, maybe three selectees, but when you put selectees together, it made for a richer experience.

There was a lot of pressure from my peers and superiors on this, including the Squadron Command Master Chief. It was suggested that I was not a team player and that it did not look good. I suggested that there was no value to it and that there was a significant downside to continuing. He was senior to me but still couldn't make me do it. I was a bit ostracized, but I persisted; alcohol was eliminated and structure put in place. I also put a structure in place around something called a charge book. I didn't invent it but knew it could be more meaningful. Its original purpose was to charge selectees with a task that they could learn from and then benefit from the written advice in the charge book as well. After completing the task from chiefs they interacted with, they would have some leadership "ah-ha" moments. It was intended to be a practical guide to be referred to for years, but with the chief's initiation, it had degraded to the point that it had no value.

For example, when I was a selectee, they sent me to a gnarly old boatswain's mate through the charge book. He was on a tugboat, and when I needed to get his signature, he wrote, "Show up, Saturday 2:00; bring two hot coffees." The coffee wasn't hot enough or strong enough when I got there. He yelled at me for fifteen minutes that he was way too busy to meet with me. We finally settled into a conversation, and I had one of the most powerful leadership discussions of my career. We talked about the responsibility of the chief and that it's not about the anchor or the title but about helping others help themselves. He is the one who talked to me about not taking care of people but teaching them to take care of themselves. He wrote in my charge book encouraging words and suggestions, and he told me if I ever said he was nice to me, he'd say I was a liar. I never forgot that conversation and the advice that was provided. I had several other great engagements and wonderful, written advice. Unfortunately, I also had disgusting things written, and even worse things put in and on the book. Long story short, my book was destroyed, and the powerful advice largely left to my memory. I changed the charge book so everyone had an opportunity as I did with that boatswain's mate, with every conversation during initiation. I also made it clear to everyone there were to be no damaging or destructive actions to the charge book in any form. Granted, there was going to be some salty language and even silly advice or charges, and that was fine. The point is the nuggets of wisdom would be honored and preserved.

| Leading isn't always easy, but it is always worthwhile when the cause is significant.

The cause must have been significant enough, because initiation has now changed to professional development and the hazing eliminated. Sometimes you are ahead of your time, and it doesn't feel right, like truly uncomfortable, but persevere; that's what leadership is about.

In our keynotes, we have a slide (picture) of a rack in a submarine situated right beside a torpedo; yes, someone will be sleeping right by the torpedo and maybe more than one if you consider hot racking. There's a picture of this rack and torpedo in the center of this book. Do you think leading people is difficult in that environment?

In the business world, leadership challenges are more similar than dissimilar. Lives aren't threatened, but that helps leaders be more effective. Emotions can be high on submarines, but in the business environment, logic and reason should rule decision-making. How do you make the changes you know you should, even when it is unpopular? And what if the changes are above your paygrade? It's still your job to influence and bridge the gap that often exists between the executive team and those that do the work at all levels. If you are that executive, how are you tapping into not only the senior levels who report to you but staying close to the mid-level managers so you can effectively make decisions for your organization?

DEEP DIVE

INTO "WHEN LEADING IS DIFFICULT"

Questions to get you thinking:

1. What are things to consider when leading is difficult?
2. What is Winston Churchill's famous quote?
3. Is failure in leadership common?
4. Is professional development more effective when it is structured?

Three things to help you navigate when leading is difficult:

1. It can be difficult being a change agent, but if it is necessary, persevere.
2. Business leaders at all levels need to stay close to the team achieving the mission.
3. When you are going through hell, keep going.

CHAPTER 9

SAILING YOUR OWN SHIP

Personal Leadership and Your Brand

You've heard the saying, "If you don't know where you are going, any road will take you there."

There are also similar nautical sayings about adjusting your sails to the winds and destination. The number one mistake leaders make is not knowing what they want in their own personal leadership. This is different than preparing for leadership in a role, although the two are often intertwined. Personal leadership is so powerful because you are totally in charge. In fact, it's probably the only thing you are totally in charge of. Leader's brands are based on human characteristics that they very consistently display.

When I consult and coach with individuals on their personal leadership, the first thing I suggest to them is to learn something about themselves they don't know. It could be through an assessment, like CliftonStrengths, DISC, Myers-Briggs, or if you have access to a 360 assessment, ask co-workers and bosses to complete a 360 for you. Getting outside your head to other's views of you will help you objectively see opportunities. After this, who knows you better than you? Sit down and do an inventory assessment of you. What are your strengths? What opportunities hold you back? In what areas could you improve on or get education, training, or personal development on that would catapult you personally?

So, what does success look like? For me, it was to know I had a plan, including goals, and that one by one, I was starting to achieve them. Before the plan, though, do you have a defined brand at home or at work?

> Are you a quiet leader or parent, open and jocular, or directed? What do you want to have as a brand of leadership that also fits who you are?

Leadership Brand

We have a popular course we teach, called "Leadership: what's your brand?" Once leaders in the course learn important facts about themselves, either through a CliftonStrengths assessment or small group discussion, we ask them to build their leadership brand and share it with others. Here's my personal brand, so you have an example of what I am talking about:

I will lead others by helping them tap into their unique talents and developing them into strengths. I will fully utilize my own unique strengths while using my core leadership characteristics of being approachable, authentic, and passionate. I commit to lifting and including all because all of us are better than one of us.

I read this, as well as the first six elements of the Gallup Q12, every day. It brings hyper-focus on the mission of continuous development of myself and others. I first learned to live by a leader's creed when I became a chief. We were almost immediately introduced to the Chief's Creed, memorized it, and adopted it as our own personal creed. Since then, I have learned the power of my own personal creed, but it all started with this:

Part of the Chief's Creed circa 1990:

> *By performance and testing, you have been advanced on this day to Chief Petty Officer. The rank of E7, only in the United States Navy, carries with it unique responsibilities and privileges you are now bound to observe and expected to fulfill. Your entire way of life is now changed. You have not just been promoted one paygrade but promoted into an elite fellowship, and as in most fellowships, you have a special responsibility to your comrades, even as they have a special responsibility to you. Your new responsibilities do not appear in print. They have no official standing. They cannot be referred to by name, number, or file. They have existed for over 100 years. Their actions and their performance demand the respect of their seniors and their juniors. It is now required of you to be the fountain of wisdom, the ambassador of goodwill, the authority in personal relations as well as in technical applications. You have made the term, "Ask the chief" a household name in and out of the Navy.*

What if each one of us lived by a creed or a statement of a brand, and in our work life and personal life, we were consistent with this brand? As you can see by my brand statement, helping people to grow is part of my DNA. My children might be frustrated with the way I suggested they grow, but developing them was very important to me, and I encouraged it in every way I could, even though at times I was not around for months. Maybe your brand is integrity, kindness, or communication. Once you have received feedback from a third party, take a stab at your own brand. Make sure to get feedback from two to three people before adopting the brand, then read it every day for sixty days, so you reinforce until it becomes muscle memory. I also suggest at some point you share this creed. Going back to accountability, posting and talking about your creed allows others to hold you accountable to your self-identified creed.

Individual Mission Plan

Once you have a clear idea of a leadership creed or brand in mind, it is time to set goals. We call these goals an Individual Mission Plan. The IMP allows you to set very specific goals that help you to prioritize those improvements that are very personal to you. The IMP is below:

What is a personal development mission? (PDM)

A personal development mission is the culmination of talents and strengths, along with those things that bring joy pointed towards dreams of achievement in any area of life.

What are the steps to the mission?

STEP 1: My personal development mission is to understand my talents through a CliftonStrengths assessment and the unique view of insights provided through the assessment.

STEP 2: My personal development mission is to analyze what makes me, me and determine what has given me satisfaction.

STEP 3: My personal development mission is to determine what my personal mission is starting with the end in mind.

STEP 4: My personal development mission is to determine what the top five goals I need to achieve are and to build my talents into a strength or determine what strengths I have through the assessment and Indicated in the insight report.

Personal Development Mission (PDM)

Name:_____ Address:_____
Current Occupation: _____ Married Y/N: __ Parent Y/N: __

My personal mission: (This could be about your career, development in the areas of parenting, partnering, leadership etc.)

_____
_____
_____

List the talents I am going to focus on to move them towards strengths

_____
_____

List the strengths and threads I can apply to achieve my mission

_____
_____

People or resources I need to achieve the mission

_____
_____
_____
_____

Personal Development Mission
Risks to achieving the mission

Time for some S.M.A.R.T. Goals
S pecific - M easurable - A pplicable – R easonable – T imeline

_____
_____
_____

Goal 1:

_____
_____
_____
_____

Goal 2:

_____
_____
_____
_____

Goal 3:

_____
_____
_____
_____

Goal 4:

_____

_____

_____

_____

Mission fully manifested:

Instructions: Using detailed and descriptive language describe what life could be like if your personal Mission is accomplished (minimum of 500 words).

_____

_____

_____

_____

_____

_____

_____

_____

Sail Off From the Safe Harbor

Once you've established a brand, obtained objective feedback to incorporate into this brand, and attempted to complete your individual mission plan, you are ready to do a personal inventory. Designing a creed first, before the personal inventory, is intended to get you to think about strengths first.

| Leaders who operate from a strength-based standpoint are more likely to feel good about themselves as leaders and to be successful as a leader.

It is likely once you've completed your creed and IMP and conducted an inventory, you will have tweaks to both documents.

All of us need mentors or coaches. I have sought out coaches my whole life as I have identified areas where I need help. Along with my other coaches, Deb and I often act as mentors to each other, consciously putting the husband/wife role aside but always asking if it is OK to share feedback. For many, that isn't possible, so look to colleagues you admire, business coaches, or bosses willing to mentor. There is richness in every relationship and good advice everywhere. Be open to listening and acting on the good advice out there.

Part of this inventory is to determine what your vision is. The vision should be descriptive of your creed and your plan. It does not have to be formal or even written, but it would sound something like this: I will drive to my organization's goals, considering people, their needs, and striving each day to achieve the most I can do, utilizing the most my team can do. Quitting is not an option.

Whatever your passion is, determination, communication, caring, competitiveness, for example, it should be described and highlighted in this vision. This doesn't so much describe your leadership creed as it does the qualities you need to achieve that creed. This is a commitment to ethics, caring, determination, or bravery but is completely unique to you. How will you accomplish the creed? Over the years, my vision of how to accomplish the creed has helped me maintain a steady course towards the leader I want to be.

While you are doing the inventory, consider whether you have experience for where you want to go or not. If you are lacking, for example, you want to be a General Manager, but you don't have finance, budgets, and strategy experience, what do you need to do?

Volunteer to work on budgets, develop a budget for a project, or maybe your mentor is from finance or has a financial background. There is always something you can do to gain experience in an area you don't have experience in. When I asked Deb how she handled this, she said most of the time, she went for the opportunity, gaining experience as she went. Whatever you do, make sure you think it through, and if you land on your feet, like Deb, go for it. Every person is different, and knowing yourself is critical to success.

Another area to consider when taking inventory is how you feel about trust and mutual respect as a leader. This trust and mutual respect not only comes from you but also sets the stage for what you expect from others. How do you react when someone does not treat you respectfully? How do you treat others? As I have said many times, the submarine environment was not always respectful, but it was direct. If I was direct with someone in the way it was done in the Navy, in my view, when they came back at me, matching comment for comment, I could not hide behind my rank, pointing to my collar. That kind of openness was my preferred way of communicating and most understood me. I also put a tremendous amount of value on trust, mine for the individual, and typically them for me. No one had to gain trust with me; it was there right away. Once lost, however, it was hard to get back. What's your trust and mutual respect inventory? Consider this and do an inventory. Are you happy with what you have found? It's hard to change human nature, but if you set an impossible standard, rethink it; it is impacting your success as a leader.

As a part of your plan to gain experience in areas where that experience lacks, consider the zig-before-you-zag plan. This was something Deb always mentioned to those she mentored. It needed to be advice to fit the individual, however. Many individuals, like Deb, are very comfortable gaining experience in a new role, but there are those that 1) are limited in moving up in their organizations (it's a pyramid towards the top for a reason), and

2) the individual is not comfortable in areas where they have no direct experience. In these two scenarios, a zig before you zag plan works. Deb has mastered this in her career planning and in advising others, and we mentioned it earlier. Lateral moves in areas of interest help you to get noticed in a new department, gain needed experience, and can be motivating to the individual. "Zig before you zag" can be a powerful tool for the right candidate.

DEEP DIVE

INTO "PERSONAL LEADERSHIP, WHAT'S YOUR BRAND?"

Questions to get you thinking:

1. What are things to consider when setting career goals?
2. What are things to consider when gaining experience in an area of interest?
3. What is important about establishing a personal standard?
4. What is your leadership creed?

Three things to navigate when establishing your leadership brand:

1. Establish a creed that you can live with.
2. Having a mentor or coach can help you be more successful.
3. Establish an individual mission plan, even if not using our document.

CHAPTER 10

SAILOR'S KNOT

Tying It All Together

We have talked about the return on investment that businesses want when they engage in the professional development of their leaders. We have talked about the return on investment of the individual who wants to grow as a leader. Leadership is critical, and the deficits associated with a lack of leadership are all around us. The benefits of positive, quality leadership are equally clear. We discussed numbers like a 30-50% improvement in key engagement areas for a company we have worked with for several months, and another client who had a low score on an initial employee survey, but on the next survey reached the top three engagement categories. Every improvement in engagement, improvements to retention, or hiring drives improvement in ROI. What does improvement in engagement do for your organization? You could see a 20% improvement in sales, a 59% reduction in turnover, and a 17% increase in productivity. What would this do for your organization in terms of revenue and achieving other financial goals? Investing in your leaders pays dividends, and once leadership is established, it never leaves us.

Strategic Takeaways for Creating Better Leaders

1. Individuals who can identify and work on their strengths are likely to have spent some time as a generalist, testing many different things in order to identify what they have talent in. There are some exceptions, for example, Michael Jordan and Tiger Woods, who showed talent and developed strengths early.
2. There is a return on investment to any individual or organization that decides to build better leadership in others and themselves.
3. Strength-based professional development contributes to significant improvements in inclusion and builds super teams we call crew-munity .
4. Setting personal goals, like an individual mission plan, helps you stay focused.

The System

You have learned the System[1] that drives inclusion:

Check-in: A system of onboarding that is so robust that upon completion, crew members (business associates) have everything they need to do their job, including tools, contacts, and familiarity with the environment. They also understand their unique contribution to the success of the mission.

Everyone Matters, if They Contribute: This is the process of identifying team members' unique contributions, providing the training to make sure they are successful, and then holding them

---

1 Patent pending

accountable for results. (We use CliftonStrengths when we can, and train associates based on their insight report.)

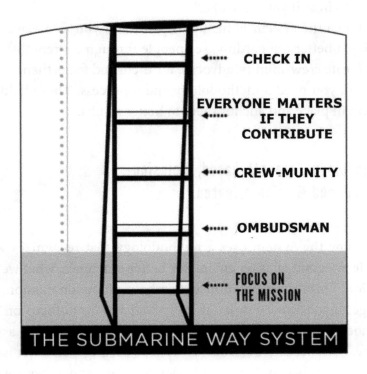

CHECK IN

EVERYONE MATTERS
IF THEY
CONTRIBUTE

CREW-MUNITY

OMBUDSMAN

FOCUS ON
THE MISSION

THE SUBMARINE WAY SYSTEM

Crew-munity: This is a healthy team wherein individual strengths blend into a synergistic fighting machine, whether the fight is for revenue, client satisfaction, or fighting the bad guys at sea.

Choose an Ombudsman: An official liaison to the Command, the ombudsman takes the pulse of the crew-munity. In the business world, the ombudsman has direct access to the most senior leaders. These individuals must be able to drive change.

Focus on the mission: This involves a clear understanding of the goals and core results needed for the organization and individuals. Do all employees, especially leaders, understand their contribution to the mission of the organization? You might be shocked at what you hear if you were to ask.

Once the system is firmly in place and you as a leader are driving a better onboarding, see people through a strength-based lens, create crew-munity, advocate for them and focus them on the mission, you need a methodology and a process. These hold the System in place and anchor them to better results.

Methodology: Strength-based, Inclusion-focused, and Mission-oriented

You know the System uses a methodology that recognizes what people are good at as an engine for better outcomes, what we call mission. This drives inclusion, but without a focus on mission, you will get inconsistent results. If every leader were to focus on this methodology, using the System to connect to people and assure their experience is good, leaders would be dealing with fewer issues caused by the backlash of poor leadership. And remember, we said leadership is a little like inclusion, a bit nebulous because building leaders is the right thing to do, but there are very few tangible steps that are recommended to drive inclusion or leadership.

You have also learned that The Five Anchors of Leadership, along with the System, the methodology and process, build better leaders everywhere. When you teach leaders while they are new to be better leaders, more inclusive leaders, they build new skills for life. On experienced leaders who don't lead this way, don't despair. Everyone wants to do what works. Leaders that lead with bias or who lack integrity or professional development can still turn it around. They must want to, and often that's because there are consequences to their action.

We have also learned about the five anchors of leadership and why these create inclusive leaders that build other effective leaders.

The Five Anchors of Leadership

Anchor 1: Fighting the submarine takes a crew-munity. Leaders are collaborative, and they encourage interdependency. They ask for input from their people and from all people where that input is value-added. This sets the stage for an inclusive leader.

Anchor 2: Captains are willing to go down with the ship. Leaders are accountable as leaders themselves and ready to go down if necessary, and they also hold others accountable.

Anchor 3: Who is your sea daddy? Leaders value continuous professional development in themselves and insist on it for others. They read books on leadership and on their area of strength and don't assume they have reached a pinnacle of anything, where learning stops.

Anchor 4: Surface with your strengths, or you will sink with your weaknesses. Leaders value what their people and others are good at. They have a way of focusing on and developing strengths. For too long, managers saw performance reviews as a time to tell people what they weren't good at. A strength-based leader manages areas of opportunity but helps their people excel and become pointy, (near-perfect performance in an area.) Becoming pointy, rather than well-rounded means interdependence and collaboration are essential. For almost everyone who becomes pointy, there is a period as a generalist, where they can identify their talents and interests and begin to build them into strengths. Building one's own strengths and appreciating other's strengths sets the stage for inclusion to happen.

Anchor 5: Crew-munity starts with crew. Leaders have caring and concern about the people they lead. They want each person to feel valued and be engaged, and the team to be better than their individual parts. Leaders are not afraid to show they care about each member of the team as an individual. They also care about the unit or team. Our motto, "All of us will always better than one of us," starts first with the individual and then caring about the crew.

CORE

The System you've heard about, along with CORE, the process that supports better leaders is:

Commitment. Leaders need to be committed to the success of every individual in the command, company, or community. Leaders show their commitment in a variety of different ways, but to make sure the System is in place is a key step.

On target training. On submarines, we drill and drill and drill. We also take professional development very seriously. If leaders are not committed to the growth of their people, engagement will be compromised. Millennials value learning and growth over latte bars and rock-climbing walls. In fact, professional development is important to every generation.

Reinforcement. Excellent training not reinforced will succumb to learning decay. 90% of all training not reinforced will be forgotten in 30 days. That is why on submarines, we drill, drill, and drill some more.

Exceptional results. If you follow the first three steps of CORE, you will get excellent results.

Good leadership takes a lot more than just five characteristics, but if a leader were to focus on the System, the Methodology, and the Process, along with the Five Anchors of Leadership, leadership itself would be instantly accelerated. As each chapter unfolded, the details of the Five Anchors of Leadership were revealed.

A client we worked with for a while, who had 100% commitment to cultural change and saw tremendous benefits in implementing the methodology, system, and process, eventually changed out critical players but was able to replace them with new talent. As the consultant leading this positive change in the organization, when it was clear the commitment was no longer there, we slowly disengaged from the client. Yes, commitment is that important.

When you learned about the Five Anchors of leadership that anchor leadership in place—yes, a bit of nautical humor—you learned that leadership is a lot more than five critical pieces, and we've elaborated on many other important leadership qualities. The Five Anchors, if learned and adhered to, assure those good leaders are in place and, even more importantly, are building other leaders to replace them.

We also discussed the symphony of leadership that is necessary for the best leadership to happen. Accountability, collaboration, interdependence, and overall leadership often must come together in a perfect symphony. We have talked about how a submarine crew of 110 on a fast attack completely turns over every three years and yet the mission is not impacted, nor is the operation of the boat itself.

We have talked about the businesses that depend on this perfect symphony of leadership without, at times, realizing the responsibility of each leader to the overall effort. How do your leaders work together to achieve goals? Do you see effective hand-offs between shifts as leadership?

You've also learned that leading can be difficult and that leaders are called upon to do unpopular things. Winston Churchill said, "When you are going through hell, keep ongoing. "

> Leadership is not about making the perfect decision. Sometimes it's about making the perfect decision for that moment.

Sometimes the decisions you make as a leader impacts one, sometimes many, and at times the call can be wrong. If the leadership decision is moral, ethical, and fair but wrong, unless it is a pattern, the leader will recover. Leading is not easy, it is not always perfect, and there isn't always a clear path, but that's what leadership is about. It is sometimes following orders others have given, making the best of it, and sometimes blazing your own trail in an area that requires situational leadership. A leader recognizes the challenge, the situation, and the team to apply to the situation and utilizes all of them to the best of their ability.

We conclude every keynote, every breakout session or workshop and every live webinar with this simple truth. Knowledge is not power; knowledge applied is power. Go through this book again, find and commit to two or three things you are going to do differently. Share those ideas with others and go do it. Reach out to us at www.thesubmarineway.com and let us begin a dialog in how we can help you and or your organization thrive. Leadership development through The Submarine Way Lens of Inclusion is changing the world. We look forward to helping you change your little piece of it.

Deb and John

CPSIA information can be obtained
at www.ICGtesting.com
Printed in the USA
LVHW011123250520
656339LV00003B/181/J